The Future of
Retail Financial Services

The Future of
Retail Financial Services

What policy mix for a
balanced digital transformation?

Sylvain Bouyon

Report of a CEPS-ECRI Task Force
Chaired by
Kim Vindberg-Larsen

Centre for European Policy Studies
European Credit Research Institute
Brussels

The European Credit Research Institute (ECRI) is an independent think tank that carries out research and contributes to the policy debate on financial services in Europe. It is managed by CEPS, a leading think tank covering a broad range of policies in EU affairs.

This report is based on the discussions and main findings in the CEPS-ECRI Task Force on The Future of Retail Financial Services, chaired by Kim Vindberg-Larsen, a FinTech entrepreneur. These findings are substantiated and elaborated via independent research carried out by the author Sylvain Bouyon, CEPS-ECRI Research Fellow, who acted as rapporteur for the Task Force.

The group met four times over a concentrated period from mid-September 2016 to January 2017. The policy recommendations put forward in this report reflect a general consensus reached by Task Force members, although not every member agrees with every aspect of each recommendation. A list of members, observers and invited guests of the Task Force can be found in Annex 1. The members were given the opportunity to comment on the draft final report, but its contents may only be attributed to the author and do not necessarily represent the views of the institutions to which the members belong.

Published by Rowman & Littlefield International, Ltd.
Unit A, Whitacre Mews, 26-34 Stannary Street, London SE11 4AB
www.rowmaninternational.com

Rowman & Littlefield International Ltd. is an affiliate of Rowman & Littlefield
4501 Forbes Boulevard, Suite 200, Lanham, Maryland 20706, USA
With additional offices in Boulder, New York, Toronto (Canada), and Plymouth (UK)
www.rowman.com

Centre for European Policy Studies
European Credit Research Institute
Place du Congrès 1, B-1000 Brussels
Tel: (32.2) 229.39.11
E-mail: info@ceps.eu
Websites: www.ceps.eu and www.ecri.eu/new

British Library Cataloguing in Publication Data
A catalogue record for this book is available from the British Library

ISBN: 978-1-78660-479-8 Hardback
        978-1-78660-480-4 Paperback
        978-1-78660-481-1 Ebook

Printed in the United States of America

Table of Contents

List of Figures

List of Tables

List of Boxes

GLOSSARY

AFM	Autoriteit Financiële Markten (Dutch Authority for Financial Markets)
AISP	account information service provider
AML	anti-money laundering
AMLD	anti-money laundering Directive
APR	annual percentage rate
ASIC	Australian Securities and Investments Commission
ASPSP	account servicing payment service provider
ATM	automated teller machine
BaFin	Bundesanstalt für Finanzdienstleistungsaufsicht (German Federal Financial Supervisory Authority)
CDD	customer due diligence
CI	car insurance
CRD	consumer rights Directive
DG FISMA	Directorate-General for Financial Stability, Financial Services and Capital Markets
DG	Directorate-General of the European Commission
DMRFS	distance marketing of retail financial services
DNB	Dutch National Bank
EBA	European Banking Authority
ECB	European Central Bank
EDPS	European Data Protection Supervisor
eID	electronic identification
eIDAS	electronic identification and trust services for electronic transactions in the internal market
ESAs	European supervisory authorities
ESMA	European Securities and Markets Authority

FCA	Financial Conduct Authority
FINMA	Swiss Financial Market Supervisory Authority
FinTech	financial technology
GAFA	Google Apple Facebook Amazon
GDPR	general data protection Regulation
IoT	Internet of Things
LIST	Luxembourg Institute of Science and Technology
MAS	Monetary Authority of Singapore
MCD	mortgage credit Directive
P2P	peer-to-peer
PISP	payment initiation service provider
PL	personal loan
PSD	payment services Directive
PSD2	payment services Directive 2
SMS	short message service
UCC	University College Cork
WP29	Working Party on Article 29 data protection

EXECUTIVE SUMMARY

While policy-makers are gradually creating the necessary conditions to strengthen the digital transformation of retail financial services, numerous policy issues and unanswered questions remain. The purpose of this report is to analyse the issues that were considered by the Task Force to be relevant for retail banking and non-life insurance at the present time and for the next few years to come. In order to develop a market in which retail financial services contribute to the economy in a balanced way, 12 main issues need to be further addressed. These issues are itemised below, followed by a more in-depth discussion of each issue, which is further elaborated in the main report.

- First, the overall regulatory framework for the digital transformation should keep consumer protection and financial stability at the core, but should also remain flexible in order to maintain a 'space of creation' for innovators.

- Second, rules that are harmonised at European level are needed for the design of so-called 'regulatory sandboxes'.

- Third, policy-makers should enact further prudential rules for peer-to-peer (P2P) platforms.

- Fourth, both policy-makers and researchers should assess to what extent the collection and use of alternative data by financial providers can benefit consumers and providers alike.

- Fifth, a satisfactory level of data privacy and quality in the used data needs to be ensured.

- Sixth, potential risks related to inclusion need to be continuously assessed and mitigated by policy-makers.

- Seventh, as regards the supervision of algorithms, policy-makers should focus on 'principle-based' rules rather than 'blacklist' rules, and should use 'second-order' supervision for enforcement.

- Eighth, noticeable updates are needed in European rules for information disclosure duties, notably in the Directive on distance marketing of consumer financial services (2002).

- Ninth, policy-makers should assess the possibility to develop a new policy model of pre-contractual personalised information disclosure.

- Tenth, more consistency is needed between the e-IDAS and pieces of legislation for financial services.

- Eleventh, the barriers to remote identification of non-residents should be thoroughly assessed.

- Twelfth, policy-makers should remove discrimination against reliance on third parties when identifying customers.

1. An overall flexible regulatory framework for the digital transformation

Firms need room for innovation and regulators should continue to organise this 'space of creation', while ensuring effective consumer protection and financial stability all along the process. In order to maintain fairness among providers, this approach should result from some combination of the two versions of level playing field ('similar product, similar regulatory treatment' and 'anyone has an equal chance of succeeding'), depending on the given environment.

2. Harmonised rules for regulatory sandboxes

So-called 'regulatory sandboxes' are attracting growing interest among some European domestic supervisors as a tool to facilitate the development of innovative solutions and monitor the digital transformation of retail financial services. These are 'safe spaces' where businesses can test innovative products, services, business models and delivery mechanisms. The development of European guidelines for national sandboxes could contribute to a convergence in domestic innovation policies across the EU, thereby facilitating the emergence of a single market for retail financial services (when one innovative product or process has been tested and approved by one domestic sandbox, this innovation could be easily assessed in any other EU country using a comparable sandbox framework). Convergence in these practices requires the creation of core European guidelines around six points: i) transparency and clarity in the rights and obligations of all the actors involved, ii) welfare of consumers at the core, iii) access for all types of suppliers, iv) a detailed list of core rules that cannot be relaxed, v) a clear exit strategy and vi) ex-post evaluation of each project.

3.   Further prudential rules for P2P platforms

The fast emergence of peer-to-peer platforms, whose business models are continuously evolving, are triggering specific risks that should require further attention from regulators. In particular, additional prudential rules that take into consideration the characteristics of these models need to be enacted. To that effect, the Task Force places some emphasis on four regulatory needs: i) risk communication, ii) orderly resolution of platform failures, iii) early warning schemes and iv) control of liquidity risks.

4.   Assessing the extent to which the collection and use of alternative data by financial providers can benefit consumers and providers alike at the different stages of the product

Benefiting from the fast growth recorded in the volume of alternative data issued by consumers (social media data, data produced by the Internet of Things, etc.), enabling technologies such as machine learning are strengthening at a steady pace, thereby gradually disrupting some aspects of retail banking and non-life insurance (as it is the case for many other sectors of the economy). Policy-makers and researchers should assess the extent to which the collection and use of alternative data by financial providers can benefit consumers and providers alike, and identify the related risks.

More specifically, research should explore how and to what extent personal data that is standardised at the global level (especially social media data) could contribute to reinforcing the single market for retail financial services. As regards advertising, customer service and retention, some focus should be placed on the role of alternative data and machine learning in reducing the amount of 'inopportune' ads and improving interactions with customers. Another core topic concerns credit scoring: to what extent and through which channels can the intensive use of alternative data enhance a balanced inclusion of the 'underbanked' and the uninsured? Finally, research should place more emphasis on how alternative data could reinforce prevention: improved anticipation of the risk of missed payments, improving fraud detection processes and greater understanding of consumer behaviour.

5.   Maintaining a satisfactory level of data privacy and quality

One of the main risks related to alternative data is that personal data of consumers are used without their clear consent and comprehension. One of the core objectives of the general data protection Regulation (GDPR), which must be implemented by May 2018, is to address this specific issue by allowing the development of standardised privacy statements that effectively and efficiently help consumers better understand the implications of the use of their data (when, how, why and where it can be used). Nevertheless, given the great diversity in the type of personal data used across the industries covered by the GDPR, the Task Force emphasises that a broad consultation should be launched by the Working Party on Article 29 data protection (WP29) and European regulators on specific elements of the GDPR, such as the mechanisms of data portability and the extent to which data breaches should be notified. Events such as the FabLab workshop, organised by the Article 29 WP, undoubtedly allow regulators to collect exploitable comments on guidelines (e.g. on data portability); nevertheless, they cannot replace proper consultation of EU stakeholders.

Another issue concerns the quality of the data used by the big data processes, even though suppliers have been given consent to use it. The incorporation of low-quality data can bias the results of the analyses, thereby resulting in two market dysfunctions: on one hand, some consumers might be unjustly discriminated against; on the other hand, errors in data can compromise the marketing and business strategies of banks. In that context, it is necessary for suppliers to assess on a systematic basis the quality and robustness of the used data.

6.   Continuously addressing the risks related to inclusion

The increasing ability of suppliers to understand the risk profile of their consumers could favour consumers with low-risk profiles and high honesty, thereby resulting in a more systematic exclusion of consumers with high-risk profiles. Policy-makers should continuously address this risk by enhancing high ethical standards in the processes used by suppliers, in line with the existing legislation adopted (e.g. mortgage credit Directive). As regards FinTech business models who promote themselves as primarily serving the 'underbanked' and uninsured, policy-makers should ensure that a balanced inclusion is achieved through these models. This implies a systematically fair use of technology (for example, to conduct an adequate creditworthiness assessment), a progressive harmonisation of rules for these new companies and the promotion of a satisfactory level of competition in these new markets.

7.   For the supervision of algorithms, developing 'principle-based' rules and 'second-order' supervision

As for the supervision of algorithms, a detailed blacklist of wrong practices might admittedly produce detailed information on what is feasible and what is not; it is likely, however, that the three core characteristics of big data (high volume, high velocity and high variety) make such an approach too challenging. In that context, policy-makers should enact general and segment-specific principles that can help shape the design of algorithms for big data.

As regards enforcement, given the increasing complexity of most algorithms, it is generally too costly in terms of time and resources for the supervisors to understand in detail the related coding and to ask for significant adjustment of the algorithm itself if necessary (the so-called first-order supervisory framework). Furthermore, such practices are likely to appear too invasive in many cases given that entire business models could be markedly affected as a result. Against that background, the favoured approach calls for supervisors to take actions that, by default, are in line with a 'second-order' supervisory framework: some of the data inputs or outputs of the algorithms that are unwanted (especially for issues related to discrimination) will have to be removed. The decision to remove data should conform to the GDPR regarding the legitimacy of the purpose for which the data is processed and the adequacy and relevance of the data used for that purpose. Such an approach will obviously imply that a proper input-outcome analysis is conducted before taking action.

For example, in order to limit the impact of certain kinds of behaviour on the pricing of health insurance, supervisors can instruct the insurer not to use the related data. As regards data outputs, supervisors can, for instance, require one provider to limit individual online search results by filtering out certain products that might not be adequate for specific consumers.

In that context, the coding of the algorithm itself does not need to be changed (if it does, this should be minor); rather, the data used and/or the results achieved need to be limited. This enforcement approach can help address the issues related to both the collection of data (in terms of privacy concerns) and the use of this data, without excessive intervention.

8.   Updates in European rules that focus on information disclosure duties

European rules focusing on pre-contractual information duties in retail financial services need to further address the new challenges resulting from the dramatic changes in consumer behaviour in recent years, especially the hybrid pattern combining online and offline interactions for the same product, and the multiplicity of devices being used. For instance, the Directive on distance marketing of retail financial services (2002) needs to be amended, notably by integrating some elements of the consumer rights Directive (2011), such as the rules on the adaptation of information requirements to technical constraints (for example, which rules to follow when there is less capacity to display the information: mobile telephone screens, SMS, etc.).

9.   Assessing the possibility to develop a new policy model of personalised information disclosure

The combination of three recent phenomena could result in a progressive transformation in the way pre-contractual information duties are designed: emergence of behavioural insights, fast growth in big data analytics and an overall consensus that standardised information disclosure policy is not sufficiently efficient. Against this background, the possibility to develop a new policy model of 'smart disclosure duties' that is personalised should be assessed thoroughly. Specifically, solutions need to be found for the six following challenges: i) voluntary basis (assent from both consumers and providers), ii) review or continuation of some core concepts of the existing European rules (such as the notions of 'average' and 'vulnerable' consumers), iii) difficulty to enforce the new rules, iv) continued risk of 'over disclosure' (notably regarding the 'privacy statement'), v) complexity of products and vi) risk of data discrimination.

10. Reinforcing the consistency between the e-IDAS and other pieces of legislation for financial services

The eIDAS Regulation (N° 910/2014) on electronic identification and trust services for electronic transactions in the internal market could have a stronger positive impact on the digital transformation of retail banking and non-life insurance if specific regulatory obstacles were overcome. In particular, there is a need to reinforce the consistency between the eIDAS Regulation and other pieces of legislation for financial services. For instance, despite the legal possibility to have digital authentication, some national provisions still oblige financial institutions to physically identify the customer in order to meet the legal requirements set out in customer due diligence (CDD) and/or anti-money laundering (AML) legislation.

11. Assessing the challenges to the remote identification of non-residents

Remote identification of the customer's identity for retail financial services is generally possible only for residents in the countries, thereby impeding the emergence of a single market for these services. Policy-makers should identify the various obstacles to remotely identifying non-resident consumers of retail financial services. One of these concerns the external information for anti-fraud purposes and for verifying customer identity that is generally available in the registers only at the national level.

12. Removing discrimination against reliance on a third party to identify customers

Whereas the objective of the e-IDAS Regulation is to focus on the identification of customers directly by remote technical means, little is said in this European piece of legislation on the identification through reliance on another party that has already identified the customer. In order to improve the efficiency of the market and enhance the comfort of consumers, the regulation of the identification through a third party should promote risk-based mitigation measures, and should not discriminate against this type of identification by placing it by default in the enhanced due diligence/high-risk AML category.

INTRODUCTION

Context

Market context

In recent years, the digital transformation of retail financial services (retail payments, current/saving accounts, consumer/housing credit, car insurance, property insurance and health insurance) has accelerated significantly. In a context of increasingly demanding consumers (in terms of digital possibilities) and rising competition, established players such as retail banks and non-life insurance suppliers are using enabling digital technologies to develop new products, processes and models. In parallel, a large number of start-ups whose main aim is to disrupt established business models through digital innovations are gradually changing the financial landscape, especially in retail payments. Finally, some companies that have traditionally been active in other sectors are showing greater interest in entering the market, in particular large information and technology organisations, such as Google, Amazon, Facebook and Apple (a.k.a. GAFA).

Legal context

This wide structural transformation is triggering specific risks that European and national regulators are gradually addressing. The range of issues is relatively broad: cybersecurity, digital interoperability, personal data protection, new norms for algorithms, contribution to further cross-border sales, digital information disclosure, etc. Ambitious regulations that are both cross-sectoral (GDPR, eIDAS, etc.) and sector-specific (PSD2, AMLD, etc.) are being implemented to address some of these issues. Nevertheless, in a constantly evolving environment, new risks will emerge during this transition period, thereby continuously challenging the adequate implementation and enforcement of established and new regulatory frameworks.

Since mid-2015, the specific digitalisation of retail financial services at large has been at the core of the policy agendas of many European stakeholders. Numerous events have been organised on this topic across Europe, by debating the related economic and policy implications. In the meantime, the number of research publications on the topic of FinTech is booming, some of them trying to influence the policy game at both national and European levels. European and national regulators have been increasingly active on the topic, with the ambition of monitoring the phenomenon without impeding it, and by analysing how and to what extent it could serve their respective agendas. The ESAs, the ECB, DG FISMA, DG Justice and DG Connect are among the European bodies that are actively working on this digital transformation of retail financial services.

Work of CEPS-ECRI so far on digital transformation

More specifically, the European Commission DG FISMA published its far-reaching Green Paper "Retail financial services: better products, more choice, and greater opportunities for consumers and businesses" in December 2015 and, in parallel, launched a broad consultation that was completed last March. DG FISMA also commissioned a large study on how and to what extent digitalisation and innovation could contribute to a single market in retail financial services (retail banking and non-life insurance). Partly based on these initiatives, DG FISMA is expected to deliver an action plan in the forthcoming months.

The study for DG FISMA was conducted by CEPS-ECRI, in collaboration with the University College Cork (UCC) and the Luxembourg Institute of Science and Technology (LIST), and included approximately 100 interviews in 11 countries (with bankers, insurers, start-ups in FinTech, large technology companies, brokers, regulators) and the organisation of four focus groups in Brussels and London (Bouyon et al., 2016). As a follow-up to the vast amount of information collected for the purpose of the study, as well as to the findings resulting from the process, CEPS-ECRI organised a Task Force that aims to discuss the policy framework for shaping the digital transformation with industry experts, regulators and academics (a detailed list of the participants can be found in the Annex).

Scope and organisation

Scope

One of the main challenges in organising a Task Force on the digital transformation of retail financial services is the sheer number and diversity of relevant topics: big data analytics, alternative data, sophisticated algorithms, machine learning, level playing field, cloud computing, financial education via digital tools, pre-contractual information disclosure in a digital context, digital authentication, blockchain technologies, overall know-your-customer infrastructures, policy package to stimulate innovation, contribution to the single market, contribution to the economic growth, impact on the labour market, shortage of adequate skills, etc. Given that the aim of this Task Force is to approach the topics with sufficient depth, members chose a limited number of issues. The choice was made based on what the Task Force deemed are and will be for the foreseeable future the most heated issues for retail banking and non-life insurance with respect to digitalisation.

Against this background, the Task Force addressed four specific core questions:[1]

- What type of level playing field is necessary during the digital transformation?

- What are the opportunities and risks related to big (alternative) data and increasingly sophisticated algorithms?

- What framework of pre-contractual information duties is appropriate in a digital era?

- How can the regulatory framework for digital authentication be improved?

Each of these questions is addressed in the following chapters. The first chapter is relatively broad and provides some insight on the type of level playing field that should be adopted throughout the digital transformation of retail financial services. In this context, some emphasis is placed on the specific regulatory needs for sandboxes and P2P platforms. The second chapter emphasises

---

[1] These four topics are deeply intertwined and are extensively related to common pieces of legislation (for example, the GDPR can have a significant impact in both chapters 2 and 3).

opportunities offered by the collection and use of alternative consumer data on different aspects of the business models of retail banks and insurers. Several key risks related to these new trends in data are then assessed and some possible solutions analysed more in detail. The third chapter concerns the potential transformation in policies of pre-contractual information duties. To better understand what is at stake, the new digital behaviour of consumers is analysed thoroughly, and a review of European rules that focus on consumer protection is conducted by determining if they adequately address the new challenges. Detailed analyses are then provided on the challenges and conditions to meet in order to develop personalised information disclosure duties. In the fourth chapter, the Task Force provides insightful analyses of the challenges and possibilities regarding enhancement of an effective digital authentication framework for retail financial services.

Methodology

The findings contained in this report are based on the outcome of four meetings organised with Task Force members between mid-September 2016 and January 2017, complemented by other relevant activities conducted by the rapporteur and the Task Force Chairman (formal interviews and informal discussions with a wide range of stakeholders, attendance at and active contribution to high-level events on the current and future implications of financial technologies, reading of academic research, etc.). In each of these meetings, high-level external experts were invited to play a part in shaping the debate on one or several of the covered issues (a detailed list of the external experts can be found in the Annex).

In line with the structure and role of CEPS-ECRI as a think tank in the European sphere, the findings published in this report in relation to the four above core topics are based on the principle of independence. This implies that the Chairman and the rapporteur have integrated the outcome of the meetings and the specific relevant activities by maintaining as much objectivity as possible. It also means that the findings contained in the report cannot define one specific agenda. Some elements corroborate some recommendations of the industry or of the consumer protection associations.[2] Others tend to promote a differentiated approach.

As such, the policy recommendations offered in this report reflect a general consensus reached by Task Force members, although not every member agrees with every aspect of each recommendation. The members were given the opportunity to comment on and discuss the draft final report, but its content may only be attributed to the rapporteur and the Chairman, and do not necessarily represent the views of the institutions to which the members belong.

---

[2] A few recommendations in this report are similar to those of other focus groups developed at European level, such as the recent Roundtable on Banking in the Digital Age set up by Commissioner Oettinger with a number of bank CEOs, sector representatives and the EBF.

1. WHAT TYPE OF LEVEL PLAYING FIELD FOR THE DIGITAL TRANSFORMATION?

The objective of this chapter is to analyse what is the most adequate policy framework for monitoring the digital transformation of retail financial services. In order to achieve this goal, analyses are first provided on the main types of actors involved in the digitalisation of retail banking and non-life insurance. Next, different versions of the level playing field are defined, in order to contribute to the development of a balanced policy framework. This conceptual framework is then applied to two different types of policy questions: How should regulatory sandboxes) be structured? How can the regulation of P2P platforms be improved? How can efficiency and fairness be ensured in both cases?

Recommendations

1. Following a case-by-case approach when assessing the regulatory needs of each segment of product, by placing financial stability and an effective protection of consumers at the core of any policy, and by combining both versions of the level playing field ('similar product, similar regulatory treatment' and 'equal chance for anyone to succeed).

2. Creating core European guidelines for the development of domestic regulatory sandboxes around the six following points: transparency, welfare of consumers at the core, access for all suppliers, list of core regulations that cannot be relaxed, a clear exit strategy and ex-post evaluation for each project.

3. Developing further prudential rules for P2P platforms that focus on four elements: risk communication, orderly resolution of platform failure, early warning schemes and control of liquidity risks.

1.1 Three main types of actors with differentiated regulatory burden

As emphasised in the study conducted by CEPS, UCC and LIST for the European Commission DG FISMA on "the role of digitalisation and innovation in creating a true single market for retail financial services and insurance" (2016), there are three types of players involved in the digital transformation of retail banking and non-life insurance:[3]

- *Established suppliers*: These include traditional banks (and their suppliers, e.g. consumer credit agencies, etc.) and non-life insurers that have already made significant innovations in their products and processes in order to face more demanding consumers, heightened competition and increasing compliance requirements.

- *New companies*: Often defined as FinTech start-ups,[4] these new entrants are typically start-ups created in recent years, which develop and distribute new processes for banks or insurance companies and/or new products for consumers (see Table 1 for a detailed classification).

- *Companies that have traditionally been active in other sectors*: These companies are examining the possibilities of disrupting retail banking, insurance, investment, capital raising, market provisioning, etc.

---

[3] See https://ec.europa.eu/info/publications/study-impact-digitalisation-eu-single-market-consumer-financial-services_en.

[4] Although the term InsurTech has become increasingly popular in recent years to define companies that disrupt the insurance sector through new technology, the present report will use the term FinTech also for insurance.

*Table 1. Different types of FinTech start-ups involved in retail banking and
non-life insurance*

	Retail banking	Non-life insurance
Products	Housing loans, consumer loans, other loans, current accounts, savings accounts, payments, others	Car insurance, property insurance, health insurance, others
Processes	**Organisation of the financial provider** Storage, archive, data collection, intermediation, others **Interactions with clients** **Pre-contractual:** marketing, advise, others **Contractual:** scoring, authentication, documentation, signature, others **Post-contractual:** Prevention, recovery, others	**Organisation of the insurance provider** Storage, archive, data collection, intermediation, others **Interactions with clients** **Pre-contractual:** marketing, advise, others **Contractual:** pricing, authentication, documentation, signature, others **Post-contractual:** prevention, fraud, claims, others

Companies in each of these groups possess strengths and weaknesses. While established suppliers can leverage both their extensive experience in providing financial services (notably with regulations) and their broad network of consumers, they also have to cope with significant legacy issues that markedly slow their digital transformation (a vast network of branches, a management philosophy that often does not match with the systematic innovative approach of the digital era, etc.) and high regulatory pressure. Owing to their small size, new companies are more flexible than established players and are more adaptable to digital changes. Furthermore, as they typically do not have banking licences, their compliance burden is much lower than for established players. Nevertheless, they also have to cope with numerous difficulties, including uneven access to funding.

Finally, companies that have been traditionally active in other sectors are showing greater interest in entering the market, in particular large information and technology organisations that can benefit from their global brands and prestige with millions of consumers (such as GAFA), as well as from their vast amounts of personal data and their technological expertise in data analytics, (open) APIs and digital interactions with consumers. Nevertheless, so far they still have low expertise in the sale of retail financial services and, should they opt to enter the market, will most likely have to comply with a vast range of banking regulations, requiring large amounts of time and resources.

1.2 'Similar product, similar regulatory treatment' versus 'equal chance for anyone to succeed'?

Limitations in the concept of 'similar'

The concept of 'level playing field' can have two definitions in business: a 'hard' version and a 'soft' version. The hard version entails that all players have to play by the same set of rules (see Arneson, 2002). The soft version implies a system where anyone has an equal chance of succeeding. Both definitions are about fairness, but the definition of fairness itself differs across the two versions. Within the hard version, respect for identical rules is fairer than the objective of giving a chance to anyone to succeed, no matter their initial characteristics and comparative advantages (size, etc.).

In theory, the hard version is approached via the key principle of *"similar product, similar regulatory treatment"*. In practice, the application of such a principle to governing a specific market of financial products proves to be rather vague, if not void. The Oxford English Dictionary defines "similar" as: "having a resemblance in appearance, character, or quantity, without being identical". In that context, the word "similar" can be interpreted in different ways and the definition of a clear perimeter might be laborious:

- *Are substitutable products systematically considered similar?* For instance, as a result of higher central bank policy rates, consumers can substitute further the holding of overnight deposits with the holding of deposits with agreed maturity.
- *Can products that target different segments of consumers be considered similar?* For instance, as shown in chapter 2, some

FinTech start-ups provide loans almost exclusively to consumers with thin credit files, while established banks focus primarily on consumers with significant financial data.

- *Can similar products a priori be eventually considered not similar if they are related to markedly different processes?* For example, P2P lending platforms providing loans as banks do are using markedly different processes to fund these loans.

The systematic application of the soft version of the level playing field, which holds that anyone deserves to have a chance to succeed, also presents significant limitations. The concept of 'equal chance of succeeding' implies that the regulatory regime can differ across providers, depending on their characteristics: size, models, etc. As is the case with the hard version, this soft approach is needed in certain circumstances, especially to prevent smaller providers from being systematically penalised due to their smaller size (smaller providers typically do not pose the same systemic risk as large providers and several research articles in recent years tend to suggest that economies of scale exist for banks in fulfilling their compliance obligations) (see Dahl et al., 2016). Nevertheless, such a softening in the regulatory burden for specific actors can only concern very specific rules.

Level playing field continuously challenged by innovation

These questions are even more challenging within the highly innovative context observed in recent years. As a result of enhanced competition and increasingly demanding consumers, both established players and FinTech start-ups are innovating continuously, and thus continuously challenging the existing regulatory framework and level playing field. In particular, in the context of the digital transformation, numerous suppliers are developing *circumventive innovations* on purpose (products and processes that are no longer within the scope of the regulation).

Retail payments is a typical market where the question of a level playing field has been markedly uncertain in recent years as a result of large-scale innovations in the sector. Lower barriers to entry, high technological content, a sector where many consumers are more prone to consume new products and the growing need for internet billing solutions caused by rapid growth in e-commerce are among the main reasons behind the high concentration of FinTech start-ups in retail payments (as presented by a representative of McKinsey at a Task Force meeting), 37% of worldwide FinTech start-ups that operated in retail activities in 2015 focused on payments. Against that background, one of the main purposes of the PSD2 (2016) was to review the PSD adopted in 2007 to take account of new unregulated types of payment services providers that have brought innovation and offer cheaper alternatives for internet payments.[5]

A case-by-case approach that places consumers and financial stability at the core of any policy

Overall, although a priori well-grounded within a theoretical perspective, the systematic application of the principle of 'similar product, similar regulatory treatment' or 'anyone has an equal chance of succeeding' entails significant limitations and risks. Against this background, the Task Force privileges a case-by-case approach that places consumers and financial stability at the core of any policy, and addresses each specific risk in a proportionate and adequate manner. In order to maintain fairness among providers,

---

[5] There was a lack of harmonisation across member states regarding the transpositions of the exemptions of a number of payment-related activities (especially payment services provided within a "limited network" or through mobile phones or IT devices). In particular, the PSD2 added two new categories of service providers, critically introducing the notion of 'push' transactions: payment initiation service providers (PISPs) and account information service providers (AISPs). The former includes payment services that are authorised by consumers to initiate payments on their behalf, bridging the merchant's website to the online banking platform of the customer to initiate payment. The latter includes aggregators of data related to consumer accounts, even if those accounts are held across many different ASPSPs. The core regulatory change of PSD2 is that banks and other payment service providers (PSPs) are required to give PISPs access to their own customers' accounts so as to facilitate transactions ordered at the customers' request. Also, PSPs have to open up access to the accounts they manage on behalf of a customer anytime these customers have provided their "explicit consent" to the (AISPs) for such access. In the meantime, both PISPs and AISPs have the obligation to comply with certain data security rules. PISPs also have to take on specific liabilities for unauthorised transactions that were under their responsibility.

this approach needs therefore to combine the two versions of level playing field, depending on the given environment.

The rest of this chapter will provide two policy examples that follow such an approach.

1.3 Further prudential rules for peer-to-peer lending

Specific characteristics of peer-to-peer platforms

Lending is the segment with the second-largest disruption (22% of the FinTech start-ups that focus on the retail market in 2015 according to McKinsey). One of the main drivers behind this dynamic concerns all the new models of peer-to-peer (P2P) lending: a pool of individuals (who are typically not professional investors) (ESMA, 2014) will lend money to the counterparty (a company or an individual) without a banking intermediary and all these investors bear part of the whole financial risk, by receiving interest on their investment from the company or individual in exchange.

The development of P2P platforms can favour financial innovation and, by increasing the number of choices for consumers, contribute to further economic welfare. As regards competition with traditional providers, Milne et al. (2016) showed that "P2P lending is fundamentally complementary to, and not competitive with, conventional banking". The core intuition behind this assumption is that P2P platforms so far have not managed to attract retail depositors and/or interbank funding within their business models, thereby implying very limited liquidity positions. According to the authors, given that P2P platforms often offer better rates for lenders, consumers most interested in funding loans on these platforms are those who can already benefit from the best rates offered by banks on products such as term deposits.

Despite providing loans as banks do, the specific characteristics of the P2P business model (specific funding channels different from banks, many consumers who are also bank customers, etc.) make the application of the principle 'similar product, similar regulatory treatment' challenging and likely counterproductive. Nevertheless, the rapid emergence of these providers, whose business models are continuously evolving, are triggering specific risks that require greater attention by regulators. In particular, further prudential rules that take into consideration the characteristics of these business models need to be enacted. The Task Force does not assess whether these rules should be passed at national or European level.

Adequate regulations of peer-to-peer platforms

Nevertheless, although P2P lending platforms still represent a very small market share of the loan market (there is a consensus that P2P platforms should represent broadly 1% of total loans by 2020; the figure could be significantly higher for consumer loans), in the current state of play, the emergence of P2P activities for the purpose of funding projects, causes or small businesses is likely to spark specific market dysfunctions that could be detrimental to lenders and borrowers alike. In particular, as emphasised by Milne et al. (2016), policy-makers should focus further on four specific regulatory priorities:

1. Risk communication

In most countries, risk communication in the P2P ecosystem is still relatively low. At best, in the UK market, high levels of disclosure are provided on historical loan default and projections of future performance (often accompanied by loan loss reserve funds). Nevertheless, little has been done so far regarding the communication of the variability of default or of loan loss recovery: in case of significant economic downturn, available reserve funds will most likely be quickly exhausted. In this context, as emphasised by the authors, a lot still remains to be done by P2P platforms on the quantification of these risks and on the information to be provided to investors regarding these risks.

2. Orderly resolution of platform failure

At present, given that P2P platforms do not qualify as typical banks, they have no obligation regarding the need to prepare plans on resolution of platform failures. One of the key arguments is that as small financial organisations, P2P platforms (even the largest ones) should not trigger any noticeable systemic risks in the event of collapse.

Nevertheless, the development of orderly resolution plans for P2P platform failure should help consolidate the activity and enhance protection of investors. In particular, as emphasised by Milne et al. (2016), P2P platforms generally have little specific internal organisation for recovering loans on a case-by-case basis and minimising post-default loan losses.

3. Early warning schemes

In line with specific domestic rules on prevention for traditional providers, P2P platforms should place further focus on early warning schemes that help them anticipate possible missed payments before they materialise. Given that P2P platforms are relatively new market players that do not offer typical banking products such as current accounts, payment services and saving accounts, they do have much less past and present financial information regarding their customers than traditional providers have regarding their own. However, P2P platforms are generally faced with less 'reputational risk' than traditional providers when developing original processes based on personal data, and they could, for instance, design early warning schemes based on alternative data (see next chapter), provided that they comply with increasing data protection requirements.

4. Control of liquidity risks

Some specific P2P platforms (especially in the US) already offer investors the possibility to readjust their exposure by selling loans to other investors on a secondary market. In this context, given the relatively low level of maturity of P2P platforms, there is potential for relatively high volatility in the interest rates of P2P platforms. As highlighted by Milne et al. (2016), a sudden rise in default rates is likely to result in lower returns; on the other hand, in case of unrelated macroeconomic shocks, returns might grow substantially and loan valuation decrease in parallel given that investors readjust their portfolio in favour of 'safer assets'. Information on potential significant volatility should be clearly provided to investors.

To conclude, as emphasised by Milne et al. (2016), an effective means to address these different risks and protect investors is standardisation. As the P2P industry gradually matures, consolidates and gets organised as a core financial activity having proper policy and strategy interests, the development of such standardisation should be progressively eased. Beyond the clear objective of curbing specific financial risks and protecting investors, the implementation of robust prudential regulation of P2P platforms across member states should contribute to enhancing the reputation of this specific sector and protecting the most reliable platforms.

1.4 Harmonised guidelines for regulatory sandboxes

Types of innovation policies

As highlighted in the previous sections, financial providers need to innovate to meet new consumer needs and tougher competition, as well as to comply with increasingly ambitious and *stringent* rules (*stringency* is the degree to which a regulation requires compliance innovation and imposes a compliance burden on a firm, industry or market). Against this background, the role of policy-makers is to develop an adequate legal and institutional framework to facilitate this digital transformation. Some combination of policy options are already being implemented in EU-28 member states, albeit with varying degrees of success: relaxation of specific compliance processes (the 'regulatory sandbox'), subsidies for innovation labs and accelerators, tax cuts, lower registration costs, financial education for techies and better access to funding for innovators (start-ups, in particular).

Each of these policy options contains pros and cons, and to a certain extent is likely to challenge the notion of a level playing field: who can benefit from it and under what conditions? Given that innovation policies by definition grant privileges (subsidies, tax cuts, etc.), a risk can emerge that such intervention will unduly favour certain actors over others. In line with the findings of section 1.2, the integration of some combination of the two versions of the level playing field should be therefore kept as a core principle of any of these innovation policies, in order to minimise as much as possible the competition distortion impact of its intervention.

Regulatory sandboxes: An infringement of the level playing field?

A new policy framework

In particular, regulatory sandboxes for FinTech, which were championed by the Financial Conduct Authority in the UK at end-2015 (FCA, 2015A, 2015B), are becoming increasingly popular around the world: Australia (ASIC, 2016), Singapore (MAS, 2016b), Thailand (Finextra, 2016) and Hong Kong (Pinsent Masons, 2016) are all taking clear initiatives to develop regulatory sandboxes for FinTech. Sandboxes are also attracting growing interest among some European domestic supervisors: the Netherlands Authority for the Financial Markets in the Netherlands (AFM) (AFM-DNB, 2016; DNB, 2016), the Swiss Financial Market Supervisory Authority (FINMA, 2016), etc. However, in some other European countries such as in France with the development of the 'soundbox' (see de Galhau, 2016), the establishment of regulatory sandboxes to enhance innovation in FinTech is currently not a priority and other frameworks based for example on a principle of proportionality are preferred.[6]

Within a regulatory sandbox, typically, one supervisor authorises one supplier to test new products and/or processes in a specific environment with lower compliance requirements and for a limited time. To a certain extent, such a framework can be analysed as an infringement of the level playing field for suppliers on the market: some market players will be protected from the regulatory burden whereas others will not. Nevertheless, in the meantime, this type of policy is also likely to offer significant advantages for accelerating the digital transformation of the retail banking and non-life insurance sectors.

---

[6] Within this framework, all companies with the same size and the same type of activity need to comply with the same rules. Technological evolution can also affect the degree to which specific companies need to comply with some rules.

Among the key advantages, sandboxes provide a safe place for firms notably to test whether their new products are complying with certain requirements and the legislative environment is adapted to the digital reality. Furthermore, supervisors can pilot the overall digital transformation by helping new entrants within the process and enabling speed of launch. The analysis of the impact should be eased significantly and allows supervisors to continuously assess the safety and robustness of the financial services ecosystem. Finally, besides enhancing the legal certainty for the participating companies and lowering the barriers to testing new products/services (companies only need to go through the full licensing procedure once they meet all criteria) that reduce compliance costs, sandboxes also allow the regulators to assess new products at an earlier phase and potentially amend legislation rapidly when beneficial to consumers.

Core principles to design balanced regulatory sandboxes

In order to be fully operational, to contain the infringement of established level playing fields and to avoid too much fragmentation across the EU-28, regulatory sandboxes should follow specific guidelines that could be enacted at European level. The development of European guidelines for national sandboxes could contribute to a convergence in domestic innovation policies across the EU, thereby facilitating the emergence of a single market for retail financial services. For instance, when one innovative product or process has been tested and approved by one domestic sandbox, this innovation could be easily approved (or rejected) in any other EU country using a comparable sandbox framework. More specifically, six core principles should be respected in order to guarantee the success of such policies and maintain a satisfactory level playing field.

1.   Transparency

A key condition for the success of regulatory sandboxes is high transparency and clarity. The respective rights and obligations of supervisors, companies and consumers during the whole sandbox period (scope of activities that can be covered by the companies, what to do in case of success or failure, etc.) need to be clearly defined and all stakeholders need to be properly informed of the conditions of the experimentation.

2. *Welfare of consumers at the core*

All new projects selected within a regulatory sandbox need to have an expected positive impact on the welfare of consumers. This positive impact on consumers' welfare needs to be one of the main criteria of selection and can be measured, for example, through the possibility to have lower prices (that can notably result from lower production/distribution costs for the industry), more comfort and security, further financial inclusion, etc. as a result of the innovation.

3. *Access for all suppliers*

In order to ensure an adequate level playing field, regulatory sandboxes need to be accessible to all types of innovative suppliers provided that they meet certain requirements. Inclusion of all suppliers is achievable only if options are available. For instance, the Dutch Bank and the AFM in the Netherlands are developing a flexible policy framework that can cover a wide range of situations (AFM-DNB, 2016):

- regulatory sandbox for both authorised businesses and non-authorised businesses,
- provisional authorisation for both authorised and non-authorised businesses and
- opt-in authorisation for pseudo banking institutions.

4. *List of core regulations that cannot be relaxed*

In order to ensure overall coherence and financial stability on the market, a detailed list of regulations that cannot be relaxed needs to be clearly defined. In order to meet this condition, several supervision authorities will likely need to be consulted (different financial supervision authorities, data protection authorities, cyber security authorities, etc.).

5. *Exit strategy*

An acceptable exit and transition strategy should be clearly defined in the event that the new solution has to be discontinued, or can proceed to be deployed on a broader scale after exiting the sandbox (MAS, 2016a).

6.   Ex post *evaluation of each project*

The competent national supervisory authority in charge of the sandbox should conduct an evaluation of each project that benefited from the sandbox environment and publish relevant evidence resulting from this evaluation. Beyond the objective of transparency, such practices can also assist supervisors in better monitoring the innovation dynamics in the segments covered. When it concerns projects that failed, relevant information on the reasons of this failure can also help market players in their innovation strategy.

2. BIG (ALTERNATIVE) DATA AND INCREASINGLY SOPHISTICATED ALGORITHMS: OPPORTUNITIES, RISKS AND POSSIBLE POLICY SOLUTIONS

This chapter focuses on the rapid development of alternative data and the opportunities, risks and possible policy solutions for retail financial services. In a first stage, some analyses are conducted in order to better understand the recent trends in source data. Next, how these trends have already affected and could affect retail banking and non-life insurance is assessed, especially by considering different European policy agendas (single market, inclusion, etc.). Finally, the main risks related to these developments and possible related policy solutions are evaluated according to four main topics: redefinition of the asymmetries of information between consumers and providers, data privacy and quality, risks regarding inclusion, and supervision of algorithms.

Recommendations

1. Assessing to what extent the collection and use of alternative data by financial providers can benefit consumers and providers alike at the different stages of the product.

2. Maintaining a satisfactory level of data privacy and quality in the used data.

3. Continuously addressing the risks related to inclusion.

4. For the supervision of algorithms, prioritising the development of principle-based rules instead of detailed 'blacklist' rules of wrong practices. Regarding enforcement, prioritising the development of second-order supervision

(unwanted input or output data of the algorithm will have to be removed, especially when it concerns discriminatory risks) rather than first-order supervision (the coding of the algorithm itself needs to be changed).

2.1 Rapid emergence of new types of data

For several decades, almost all the information used by financial organisations and insurance companies in the different phases of the product (advertisement, scoring, pricing, prevention, etc.) has been structured data. In the present analysis, this type is defined as data generally stored in a relational database and that can be easily mapped into pre-designed fields. Typically, payment providers, lenders and insurers (the traditional providers) have collected and combined structured data originating internally and/or externally.

Internal structured data can concern, for example:

- Standard customer information: age, owner/tenant, marital status, number of children, etc.
- Financial flows and financial balances contained in the current accounts of in-house customers

External structured data can concern, for example:

- Databases produced by credit bureaus
- National car insurance databases built by a consortium of domestic insurers to track licence plates, driver identity, stolen or written-off vehicles, accident claims, etc.
- Data structured by telecommunication companies, utilities, etc.

Nevertheless, in recent years, new types of data have been rapidly emerging and are gradually disrupting the sectors of retail financial services and insurance. These new types are defined as 'alternative data' in the present study. They can concern, for example:

- Social media data (as shown in the box below, it has grown tremendously since 2010)
- Data produced by the Internet of Things (IoT): telematics for car insurance, smart home solutions for property insurance, fitness trackers for health insurance, etc.
- Data issued by smartphones

Contrary to the 'traditional' data used by mainstream providers, a significant part of this emerging data is unstructured.[7] This information is not stored in a traditional row-column database and often includes text and multimedia content. As with structured data, it can be collected internally (Word documents used for procedures, emails of employees, etc.) or externally (SMS for private usage, etc.). Below is a non-exhaustive list of the sources of unstructured data that financial/insurance providers can (or could) use when they arrange the pre-sale, sale and/or post-sale of their products:

- conversation, pictures and videos from social media sites such as Facebook, Twitter, Google+ or Instagram
- data from surveys and market research
- data from ATMs or call centres
- data from emails, SMS, any other types of messages or documents
- data from consumers' complaints and feedback
- data from sensors
- websites

---

[7] A third group includes semi-structured data, which are not stored in a relational database but do have some organisational properties that make it easier to analyse (such as tags or other markers to separate semantic elements, and it enforces hierarchies of records and fields within the data). Examples of semi-structured data might include XML documents and NoSQL databases.

Box 1. Rapid growth in the volume of digital unstructured data created by consumers

The volume of digital unstructured data created by consumers has increased immensely in recent years.[8] In 2015, this type of data should reach broadly 5.4 exabytes, whereas the total amount of digital unstructured data stood at only 1.1 exabytes in 2010 (see Figure 1). In parallel, social media penetration among the population has also increased tremendously. For example, according to the Pew Research Centre, the share of the US adult population connected to the Internet and using social networking has increased markedly since the early stages of social networking (see Figure 2). As expected, the 18-29 age group was the first to grow and by mid-2008 two-thirds of those of this generation that were connected already used social networking. It took more time for all generations to pass half of the related online population, but by mid-2015 all age groups had at least half of their online population using social networking: 92% of 18-29, 81% of 30-49, 67% of 50-64 and 56% of over-65. Figures are likely to be broadly similar in Europe, albeit with differences across countries.

Figure 1. Volume of digital data stored

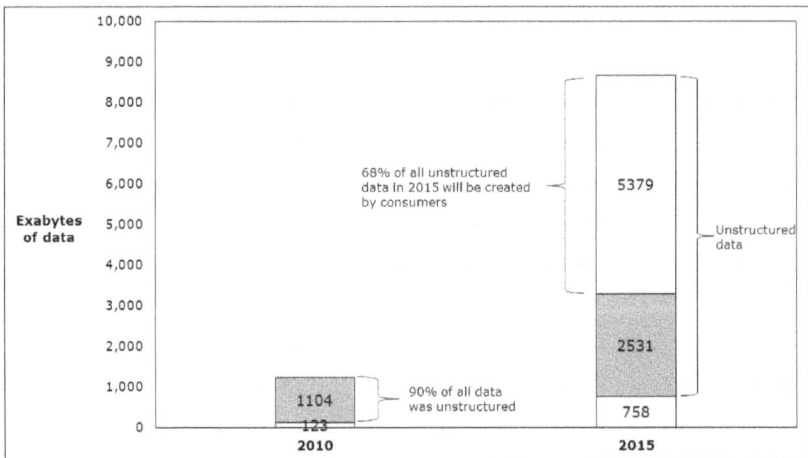

Notes: 1 Exabyte (EB) = 1 million Terabytes (TB). For context, Facebook ingests 500 YB of data each day.
Source: International Data Corporation, BI Intelligence Estimates.

---

[8] Contrary to structured data, unstructured data cannot be organised in typical relational databases.

Figure 2. Social networking use (% of Internet-using adults, 2005-15)

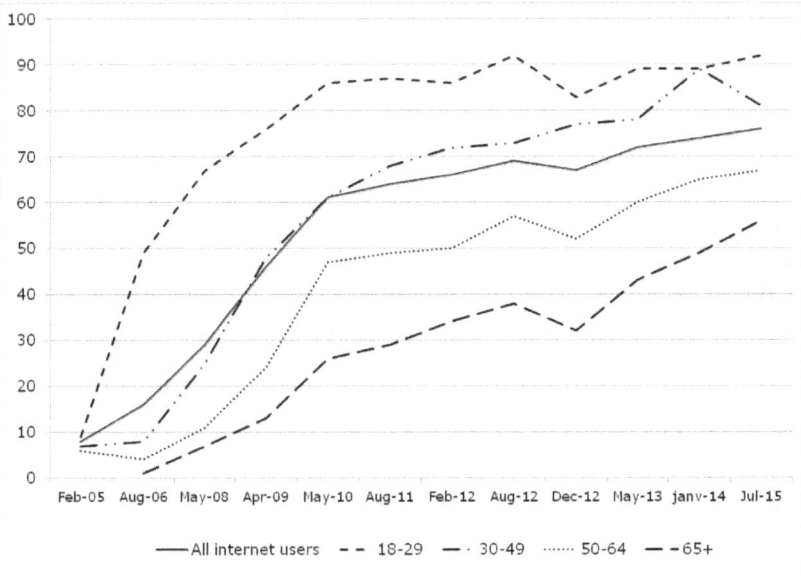

Source: Author based on data from Pew Research Centre.

2.2 Opportunities for retail financial services and insurance

Enabling technologies such as machine learning are strengthening at a steady pace,[9] especially by benefiting from the rapid growth recorded in the volume of alternative data. These types of data are already used to a significant extent by a growing number of FinTech start-ups that offer services to the final consumers. Furthermore, a

---

[9] Machine learning is a discipline combining science, statistics and computer coding that aims to make predictions based on patterns discovered in data. As opposed to rule-based decision systems, which follow an explicit set of instructions known in advance by developers, machine learning algorithms are designed to analyse data and discover patterns that people cannot find by themselves. In other words, machine learning leverages the massive power and objectivity of computers to see things in big data that comparatively slower and biased humans cannot, and then use those insights to determine how new data can be used to accurately predict results.

good many of traditional providers are already testing the use and, for a few of them, even using this alternative data.

The disruption of certain aspects of the core businesses of traditional providers is likely to heighten in the near future, especially as the number of FinTech start-ups that develop new big data processes keeps increasing. The intensity of the impact of this new data can differ across the types of consumers and phases of the product, but overall the stated objective of using such data is to further personalise the services and place the customer at the centre of the relationship. The introduction of such data has the potential to help traditional providers more effectively meet consumers' needs, thereby contributing to the enhancement of their overall welfare. However, its use can also trigger specific risks that will be assessed in section 2.3.

Opportunities regarding the reinforcement of the single market

Regardless of the phase in which providers integrate social media data, one of the main characteristics of this type of data is its global standardisation. Companies such as Facebook, Twitter, LinkedIn, Instagram, Google+, etc., are global brands that have shaped their tools in a similar way all around the globe. For instance, the layout and available functions of Facebook are standardised at a world level. Anyone can decide if he "likes" or "does not like" a post, anytime, anywhere.

In this context, should some financial companies develop specific solutions in a domestic market by processing social media data, such solutions could be easily replicated in other countries, on condition that the company has the authorisation to use this local social media data and has sufficient resources at its disposal to integrate foreign languages. Therefore, the main challenge to the development of global solutions based on social media data is likely to concern primarily the differentiation in local data compliance rules rather than the way this personal data has been structured. Provided that suppliers can overcome the differentiation in local data compliance rules and cope with different languages, the extensive use of alternative personal data could contribute to reinforcing somewhat the single market for retail financial services.

Advertising, customer service and retention

Advertising is often perceived as the main and sometimes only channel through which data from social media and the Internet of Things has the potential to influence markedly the offer of retail financial services. Although such data can disrupt other phases of the product, it is nonetheless true that the traditional way of conducting marketing campaigns could be overhauled by increasingly sophisticated algorithms that could do the best of this data. This approach should result in more refined segmentation of the targeted consumers and better perception of their aspirations. Against this background, providers could better understand when, where and how their brand could be relevant, thereby resulting in more targeted advertising and reducing the amount of 'inopportune' ads.

Different approaches are already at the disposal of providers to make the best of this data. For instance, technologies such as machine learning can follow a "social semantics" approach: sometimes called "deep learning", machine learning is the processing of large datasets and can be compared to a neural network recognising abstract patterns. Through the use of social media conversations in different countries, the emotional and social factors individuals consider when making borrowing or insurance decisions can be better understood and the marketing campaign markedly refined.

An increasing number of traders are developing part of their customer service and strategy of retention by adding some of the social media platforms as a permanent channel for retail customer interaction, fully integrated into relationship management systems. Within this process, it is expected that both providers and consumers can learn by exchanging on forums about brands and services. Providers can, for example, assess the success of their service and where it could be improved. By reading about the shared experiences of other consumers, consumers can use these forums as a source of advice on products, as a complementary or substitute to traditional word of mouth. Nevertheless, owing to the significant risk of fraud and still low percentages of consumers sharing their purchase experiences with other consumers online, traditional suppliers are using these platforms on a marginal basis, at best.[10]

Contractual phase: What are the opportunities in terms of credit scoring?

Although alternative data appears a priori less relevant to the contractual phase than to the advertisement phase, there are also significant opportunities in the use of alternative data for creditworthiness and insurance pricing. Some rapidly growing FinTech start-ups have been developing business models that rely on machine learning aimed at processing any type of data, including social media, to score consumers and provide them with loans if they receive a satisfactory creditworthiness assessment (some examples have been spotted in Poland, Spain and the UK).

As often emphasised by this type of loan provider, these scoring techniques based on social media data could allow more underbanked persons to access the credit market. One of the key drivers behind this trend is that many of these underbanked have too little past financial data and their thin credit files often do not allow traditional providers to conduct adequate creditworthiness: young households, recent migrants, etc. According to a significant number of actors on the market, the steady growth in social media data is likely to be a game changer for this segment of households. Nevertheless, as assessed in section 2.3, several key issues and risks will need to be addressed further by policy-makers.

---

[10] As revealed notably by the Google Barometer Customer Survey (2015), the exchange of experience of a brand on social media networks differs significantly across countries. For instance, in the case of personal loans, this survey revealed that the share of consumers who shared purchase experiences on social networks stood at 19% in the UK, 15% in the Netherlands, 12% each in Italy and Belgium, and 11% in Germany, whereas it reached only 2% in Finland and 2% in Estonia (for car insurance, the share was 17% in the UK and 8% in both Poland and Sweden, and below 4% in Finland, Estonia and Belgium). The findings of the Google Barometer can be found in: www.consumerbarometer.com/en/.

Box 2. New models of credit scoring

Traditional scoring is based on 'standard' data (collected in-house or externally) and a standard hypothesis (for example: "people with unlimited working contract and real estate property repay better").[11] The use of big data analytics and machine learning implies that the model becomes self-learning as to the impact of existing and new data, implying that the scoring model changes constantly (with continuous correction to ensure that correlation holds over time and across data). Each new repaid or defaulted loan changes the acceptance criteria for the next marginal loan underwriting. The latter methodology is based on the massive amount of data available and can integrate any type of unexpected correlations (see www.kreditech.com). For example, some correlations could show that some consumers who were not repaying in the first model had a font installed on their computer from casino and poker software.

Contractual phase: How could new practices of insurance pricing using alternative data improve the quality of the insurance products?

As regards insurance providers, the approach in terms of big data to price products can be broadly similar; however, it can have further-reaching consequences. Based on a logic of risk-pooling, traditional insurance pricing allows for minimising the cost impact of the higher-risk individuals by insuring consumers who are unlikely to need insurance. The analytics performed by actuaries, based on advanced mathematical and financial models, have traditionally aimed at improving insight into individual policyholder risk characteristics to distinguish good risks from the bad and to accurately price each risk accordingly. Big data that includes, for example, information produced by telematics in cars allows for better understanding of the driving behaviour of the insured and should raise the predictive power of the models. In this context, increasing refinement in risk assessment should result in smaller and more predictable risk pooling, thereby contributing to fairer insurance pricing that depends further on the true individual risk profile.

---

[11] Further analyses on these new models can be found on the website of the company Kreditech at www.kreditech.com/.

Post-contractual phase: How could alternative data contribute to further emphasis on prevention?

In recent years, encouraged notably by specific domestic regulatory requests, traditional providers have gradually created processes that further enhance prevention. For example, on the credit market, an increasing number of traditional providers have developed early warning schemes: based generally on traditional structured data, these schemes allow for anticipating the risks of future late payments of each consumer. Such an approach places more emphasis on early detection by allowing possible arrangements before the missed payments materialise, rather than on late detection, recovery constraints and possible litigation. The use of alternative data and machine learning that assess the risk of non-payments on a regular and continuously updated basis is already used by specific FinTech platforms. For example, better knowledge on the personal and professional evolution of their customers via their social media activities can help anticipate the risk of future missed payments.

The role of big data should be even important for insurance markets, as it could in theory emphasise prevention through two channels. First, the 'behaviour approach' implies that insurers have better knowledge on the behaviour of consumers thanks to the significant growth in alternative data produced by sensors, etc., and can, for example, offer a lower premium on the condition that consumers adjust their behaviour in order to alleviate risks (through driving lessons for car insurance, better diet and sleep for health insurance, etc.). On the other hand, big data analytics should improve fraud detection processes. The use of social network analytics that assumes that fraudulent consumers are more likely to be connected with other fraudulent consumers helps better identify fraudsters.[12] This should result in decreasing fraud costs for both providers, as they do not have to cover the cost of accidents based on false claims, and non-fraudulent consumers, as average premiums should decrease and insurers do not need to systematically investigate in detail their claims/fraud presumption.

---

[12] For a more detailed analysis on the use of social network analysis in the detection of fraudsters, see www.iabe.be/sites/default/files/bijlagen/big_data_paper_full_v009.pdf, pp. 12-13.

2.3 Risks for retail financial services and insurance, and possible regulatory responses

The increasing use of alternative data contributes to a progressive change of philosophy and approaches, bringing numerous opportunities for consumers and providers, but also triggering new types of risks. The objective is to assess the types of risk specifically triggered by the use of big alternative data in retail banking and non-life insurance, and to determine the most adequate regulatory option to mitigate them.

The policy objective of promoting fairness in the use of personal data needs to address risks according to four main topics:

- redefinition of the asymmetries of information between providers and consumers,
- data privacy and quality,
- risks regarding inclusion and
- supervision of algorithms.

Redefinition of the asymmetries of information between providers and consumers

A significant part of policies conducted at European or national level are intended to correct dysfunctions that may occur in the structure of retail financial services. In particular, some of the main dysfunctions concern the asymmetric information that can be present on both the providers' and consumers' sides. At present, owing to their greater experience and knowledge of the financial products they are in charge of selling, providers are expected to possess more information on the features of the products than consumers possess. As a result, some of these providers might have incentives to exploit existing asymmetries of information to boost revenues by selling products which are not necessarily in the consumer's best interest (moral hazard).

On the other hand, consumers typically possess more information on their financial situation or the risks they are taking than the providers have. As a consequence, even though they are likely to be aware of potential difficulties in reimbursing loans or their excessive risk-taking behaviour in the context of an insurance contract, some consumers may be prone to provide a biased assessment of their own situation in order to contract products.

The increasing amount of available data and sophisticated algorithms is contributing to transforming these different market dysfunctions, hereby leading to a redefinition of the balance of information asymmetries between the consumers and providers. In principle, by using different digital platforms, such as comparative websites or social media forums, consumers should be able to understand better the products offered to them, hereby contributing to alleviating the asymmetric information that is detrimental to them. However, the main effect of big data should a priori concern the second type of asymmetric information: based on machine learning processes and big data analytics that include alternative data, providers can develop a much deeper knowledge of the risk profile of each of their consumers.

This expected new state of play implies that adequate scrutiny needs to be ensured by policy-makers, given their relatively limited amount of resources to address the issues sparked by big (alternative) data. One possibility for 'rebalancing' the information asymmetries is analysed in chapter 3 with the development of 'personalised' pre-contractual information duties that should assist each consumer in better understanding the features of the products.

Data: Privacy and quality

1. Privacy: Violation of confidentiality agreement presumed at disclosure

Significant issues can appear when consumer data are passed on to the secondary market for big data. The recently enacted reform of data protection rules in the EU (GDPR) should help reinforce privacy rights and decrease the differentiation in personal data protection across member states in the coming years (to be implemented by May 2018). If specific rules such as the "right to be for forgotten and to erasure" (European Commission, 2012: Art. 17), "easier access to your own data",[13] the "right to know when your

---

[13] See European Commission (2012: Art. 14). In the context of the concept of "easier access to your own data", individuals will have more information on how their data are processed and this information should be available in a clear and understandable way.

data has been hacked"[14] and "the right to data portability"[15] were sufficiently harmonised across the EU-28, consumers might notably feel more comfortable to engage in cross-border sales of financial products with marketing or/and scoring based on their personal data.

Nevertheless, given that the GDPR is a multi-sectoral regulation and that there is great diversity in the type of personal data used across the industries covered by the GDPR, the Task Force believes that a broad consultation should be launched by European regulators to clarify some specific elements of the GDPR, such as the mechanisms of data portability, the definition and implication of data ownership across industries and the extent to which data breaches should be notified. This process is essential to ensure an efficient implementation of the GDPR in retail financial services, by allowing the development of standardised privacy statements that truly and efficiently help consumers better understand the implications of the use of their data (when, how, why and where it can be used). This is especially important for new FinTech business models that primarily target the traditionally underbanked and uninsured, since a likely higher share of these consumers has little concern for what is done with their personal data (see above in the sub-section "contractual phase").

2.   Quality: level of accuracy in data

Privacy issues as discussed above concern the rights of consumers regarding the use of their personal data and might be primarily based on the harmful impact of big data practices resulting from the use of information for which consent has been provided. Another issue concerns simply the quality of the data used by the big data processes. The incorporation of low quality data, which suppliers

---

[14] See European Commission (2012: Arts 31 and 32). The "right to know when your data have been hacked" means that, for example, companies and organisations must notify the national supervisory authority of serious data breaches as soon as possible so that users can take appropriate measures.

[15] See European Commission (2012: Art. 18). The "right to data portability" means it will be easier to transfer your personal data between service providers.

are permitted to use, can bias the results of the analyses, thereby possibly resulting in two market dysfunctions: on one hand, some consumers might be unjustly discriminated against; on the other hand, errors in data could compromise bank marketing and business strategies.

As emphasised by Martin (2015), many data sources may be undesirable because of the quality of the information and biases in the data: for example, these biases can skew it toward specific types of users, such as on the basis of race, ethnicity, gender, socioeconomic status or location. This poor quality may be an issue due to inaccuracies in the data or a lack of coverage. Inaccuracies may arise from the manner in which the data was collected, the degree of imputed data within the data source or from deliberate obfuscation by users (for example to shape social media data that can be used by suppliers). In this context, it is necessary for suppliers to assess on a systematic basis the quality and robustness of the data.

Risks regarding inclusion

1. Exclusion of more risky consumers ('behavioural discrimination risk')

Provided that firms do not try to take advantage of the first type of information asymmetry and adequately address the needs of consumers, their increasing ability to understand the risk profile of their consumers could favour consumers with low-risk profiles and high honesty, thereby triggering a so-called 'behavioural discrimination risk'.[16] The argument that consumers' honesty could be enhanced within this system cannot be disregarded. Nevertheless, consumers with higher-risk profiles could be excluded on a more systematic basis from retail banking and non-life insurance markets (due to continuously refined pooling). Behavioural discrimination risk will need to be continuously addressed by regulators by, for example, enhancing ethical

---

[16] Another possibility is that as big data allows for better targeting of customers, traditional providers that use these processes could propose more adapted products.

standards (for an overview of the concept of behavioural discrimination, see e.g. Ezrachi & Stucke, 2016).

2. How to enhance a balanced financial inclusion with new FinTech business models?

As analysed in the sub-section on the contractual phase, the steady growth in the volume of personal data, such as from social media, could contribute to reinforcing financial inclusion of the underbanked. Nevertheless, questions remain on the type of financial inclusion that can be enhanced by such practices, and these questions might require some policy intervention at a later stage. A possible definition of "balanced financial inclusion" refers to access and use of financial services, provided by mainstream providers (in the meaning of "non-stigmatising, because dedicated to poor or vulnerable people"), that fit the needs of the consumer in the environment in which he or she is living, without excessive risk of missed payments.

Given that FinTech start-ups that assess the creditworthiness of consumers through the use of alternative data have only been created in recent years, there is so far little evidence that such practices consistently result in a fair use of this technology. In addition, depending on their status and the country where they operate, these FinTech start-ups are likely to benefit from less constraining regulations than traditional providers are. Further policy intervention might therefore be needed in the coming years to ensure proper consumer protection in these specific segments. Finally, a satisfactory level of competition should be promoted in these segments in order to ensure a reasonable level of choice and affordability for consumers who use that type of service.

Supervision of algorithms[17]

1. Principle-based rules versus blacklist rules

The emergence of big data, particularly in the retail financial services sector, has triggered the specific risks highlighted so far.

---

[17] Some important issues related to the supervision of algorithms have not been discussed in the Task Force. For example, the question of the

Due to its rather nascent attributes, the big data 'industry' still has few norms or supply chain best practices that can guide it. Specific rules that provide such norms are already needed and will help the big data sector structure the scope of its practices and targets. Documents such as Opinion 4/2015 of the European Data Protection Supervisor, which emphasises the application of principles such as fairness and legitimacy, are essential in this respect (EDPS, 2015). Although principle-based regulations might result to ambiguities in certain circumstances, they seem to be more appropriate than a blacklist approach.

A blacklist approach admittedly allows for detailed information on what is feasible and what is not; however, the three core characteristics of big data (high volume, high velocity and high variety) likely make such an approach too challenging. Blacklisting in the case of big data will indeed require a significant amount of resources from supervisors, as such lists might be long (and hardly exploitable by providers) and will require continual adjustments.

General principles that can contribute to shape the big data industry and its design of algorithms can be, for example:

- Any new algorithm works in the interest of consumers.
- Strong security measures are systematically designed in order to prevent data breaches.
- Correlations do not systematically imply causation (for example, belonging to a particular ethnicity does not systematically entail a low income).
- The design of the algorithm itself does not have any discrimination content (discrimination risk, if any, can only result from the use of biased data).
- The objective and general operating of one algorithm can be explained in understandable terms to consumers (in conformity with the GDPR).

Some specific principles can be added to cover the design of algorithms for particular segments of products. For instance, when

---

copyright of algorithms will become one of the key matters in the coming years and could be analysed in more detail in other CEPS-ECRI research activities.

designing algorithms that aim at assessing whether a consumer can be granted a loan, specific principles can be included, such as:

- Creditworthiness assessment should pursue its initial purpose: to determine whether a consumer can comply with payment requirements within the duration of the credit, without particular hardship. The result of the assessment of creditworthiness is "Yes", "No" or "more information is needed before completing the assessment".

- That assessment of creditworthiness should take into consideration all necessary and relevant factors that could influence a consumer's ability to repay the credit over its lifetime.[18]

- Credit risk refers to the risk borne by the creditor and the probability and size of a loss due to a credit awarded. Expected loss of the creditor may be reduced by personal guarantees. This is irrespective of the consumer's ability to repay.[19]

2. *'First-order' supervision versus 'second-order' supervision*

One key question remains regarding the way supervisors can take action to enforce specific rules or ensure that some practices are in line with the enacted core principles. In the rapid development of

---

[18] This principle can be found in the Mortgage Credit Directive, Recital 55. The objective of creditworthiness assessment with respect to Directive 2008/48/EC is clearly indicated in the Judgment of 27 March 2014 of the European Court of Justice C-565/12 in the following terms (para. 42): "since the creditor's obligation, prior to conclusion of the agreement, to assess the borrower's creditworthiness is intended to protect consumers against the risks of over-indebtedness and bankruptcy". The Judgment of the European Court of Justice C-449/13 of 18 December 2014 (Consumer Finance) confirms that the burden of proof of non-performance of creditworthiness assessment lies with the creditor and, moreover, the interpretation of the Directive 2008/48/EC "precludes national rules according to which the burden of proving the non-performance of the obligations laid down in Articles 5 and 8 of Directive 2008/48 lies with the consumer".

[19] According to FinCoNet, it is a risk to the credit provider of entering into a 'bad loan', i.e. with the likelihood of a consumer defaulting or being unable to repay their loan obligation.

big data, supervisors have to cope with two severe constraints: technical skills and resources. In order to deal with these two constraints, supervisors need to have sufficient in-house skills to understand the inner workings of the supervised processes and sufficient resources to supervise properly by taking action, if needed. To a certain extent, the constraints are intertwined.

Given that an increasing number of processes are complex algorithms that notably structure machine learning methods, it is generally too costly in terms of time and resources for the supervisors to understand the related coding and to ask for an adjustment of the algorithm, if necessary. Furthermore, such practices are likely to appear too invasive in many cases given that entire business models could be markedly affected as a result. Therefore, as highlighted by Wagner (2016), one possibility is to occasionally introduce case-by-case filters in order to modify the *prima facie* responses of the system. In this context, a distinction needs to be made between 'first-order' supervision and 'second-order' supervision. The former implies that supervisors require the business to change the coding of the algorithm itself in order to comply with the regulation. Within the latter supervisory framework, data inputs or outputs of an algorithm has to be limited without actually changing the algorithm itself.

The privileged approach is that supervisors by default take actions that are in line with a second-order supervisory framework: some of the data inputs or outputs of the algorithms that are unwanted will have to be removed (especially to address risks of discrimination). The decision to remove data should conform to the GDPR regarding the legitimacy of the purpose for which the data is processed and the adequacy and relevance of the data used for that purpose (see Recital 39 of this regulation).[20] Such an approach will obviously imply that a proper input-outcome analysis is conducted before taking action.

---

[20] In particular, the Recital 39 stipulates that:

The specific purposes for which personal data are processed should be explicit and legitimate and determined at the time of the collection of the personal data. The personal data should be adequate, relevant and limited to what is necessary for the purposes for which they are processed.

For example, in order to limit the impact of certain behaviours on the pricing of health insurance, supervisors can instruct the insurer not to use the related behavioural data. A similar supervisory approach can be adopted regarding loans when some providers assess the creditworthiness of a specific consumer by using the financial situation of the users included in his Facebook network (some of these practices are likely to result in discriminatory selection).[21] As regards data outputs, supervisors can, for instance, require one provider to limit individual online search results by filtering out certain products that might not be adequate to specific consumers.

In this context, the algorithm itself does not need to be changed in depth, rather its results simply need to be limited. This approach can help address the issues related to both the collection of data (in terms of privacy concerns) and the use of this data, without excessive intervention.[22]

---

[21] Other examples of data inputs that can be unwanted can be found on page 22, point 40 and page 23, point 41, of the ESA's Joint Committee Discussion Paper on the use of big data by financial institutions (2016).

[22] Nevertheless, it is worth mentioning that in some cases, limiting the input could mean that the algorithm is not effective anymore.

3. WHAT SHOULD BE THE FRAMEWORK FOR PRE-CONTRACTUAL INFORMATION DUTIES IN A DIGITAL ERA?

The core objective of this chapter is to assess how the established model of pre-contractual information duties could be improved in a digital environment. For that purpose, statistical analyses are first conducted in order to better appreciate the recent trends in distribution channels. Then, a detailed review of online aspects in existing European rules for pre-contractual information duties is carried out. Finally, the possibilities and challenges of a model of pre-contractual personalised information duties are analysed in details.

Recommendations

1. Updates in European rules that focus on information disclosure duties (notably the Directive on distance marketing of consumer financial services, 2002), by systematically taking into consideration the four following elements: high online distribution shares, significant omnichannel approach in consumer behaviour, different distribution devices involved, and significant differentiation in the pace of digital transformation across countries.

2. Assessing the possibility of developing a new policy model of 'smart disclosure duties' that is personalised. In order to do so, it is necessary to assess the possibility to develop solutions to the six following challenges: voluntary basis, review of some core concepts of the existing European rules, difficulty to enforce the new rules, risk of 'over-disclosure', complexity of products and risk of data discrimination.

3.1 The big picture: some statistics on the online/offline behaviour of consumers

First awareness and research phases: High online share

Scant data is available on the use of online or offline distribution channels to purchase financial services. In 2015, based on a broad survey of consumers, Google published vast amounts of data on distribution channels for personal loans (PL) and car insurance (CI). As shown in Figure 3, the unweighted average market shares of online and offline channels for first-time awareness and research by consumers for personal loans and car insurance was as follows:[23]

- First-time awareness of consumers (via website or application): 55.2% (PL) and 64.4% (CI)

- Research (only online research): 17.1% (PL) and 33.3% (CI)

- Research (only offline research): 19.1% (PL) and 16.9% (CI)

- Research (compared products/prices/features online): 37.2% (PL) and 63.4% (CI)

Given that one decade ago online channels were almost non-existent, the digitalisation of the interactions between providers and consumers has been spectacular. These rapid developments are mainly due to deepening Internet penetration into the habits of the European population at large (as shown in chapter 2 on the use of alternative data). Nevertheless, the intensity of the digitalisation of distribution channels varies significantly across both products and phases:

- *Products*: There are significant differences between car insurance and personal loans: for instance, the share of consumers that compares products/prices/features online reached 37.2% for personal loans and 63.4% for car insurance.

- *Phases*: Whereas 55.2% of consumers had first-time awareness via website or application for personal loans, 17.1% of them used only online research.

---

[23] This unweighted average includes Belgium, Estonia, Finland, France, Germany, Ireland, Italy, the Netherlands, Poland, Sweden and the UK.

High online shares are a game changer for policy-makers, since most European regulations on consumer protection were enacted before the rapid increase in digitalised distribution channels.

Figure 3. Distribution channels for different products: Consumer research (2015, % of total)

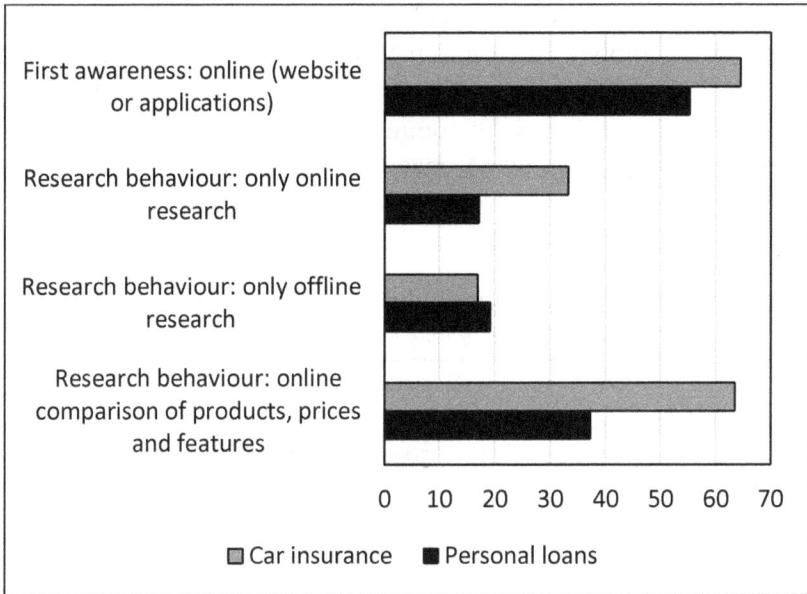

Source: Author based on data from Google Consumer Barometer Survey (2015).

Research and purchase behaviour: Omnichannel approach

As regards the distribution channels for research/purchase of financial products, the share of online and/or offline interactions is as follows:

- Research/purchase (research online/purchase offline): 41.1% (PL) and 32.8% (CI).
- Research/purchase (research offline/purchase online): 20.8% (PL) and 4.7% (CI).
- Research/purchase (research offline/purchase offline): 51.5% (PL) and 31.5% (CI).
- Shared purchase experiences on social network(s): 9.1% (PL) and 5.6% (CI).

One of the key trends reflected by these statistics is the rapid emergence of the omnichannel approach, where financial/ insurance providers develop cross-channel business models. In order to purchase car insurance or secure a personal loan, a significant share of consumers adopt a hybrid online-offline behaviour pattern, as their interactions with the products and the providers result from some combination of digital and non-digital elements. As shown above, and below in Figure 4, this is especially true for the combination of online research and offline purchase.

Increasing shares of omnichannel behaviour can pose significant difficulties when enacting consumer protection rules, since regulations need to cover both online and offline channels for one specific contract.

Figure 4. Distribution channels for different products: purchase and post-sale phase (2015, % of total)

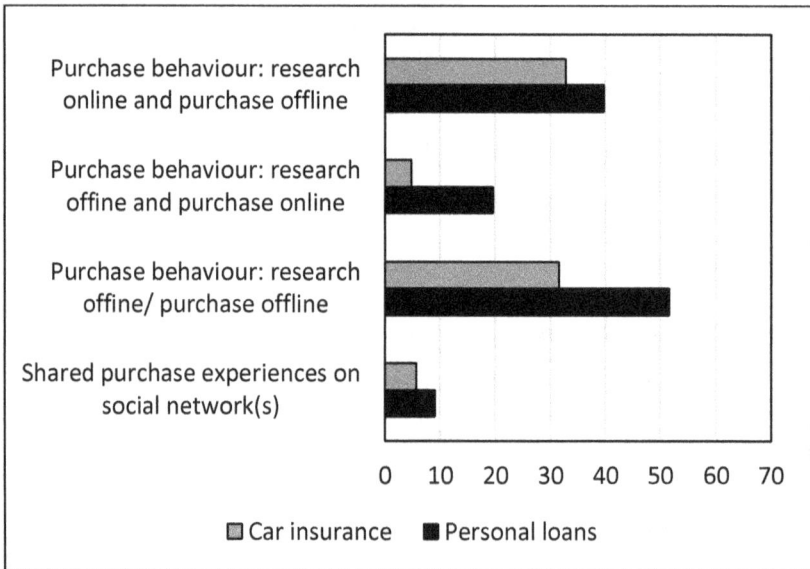

Source: Author based on Google Consumer Barometer Survey (2015).

Differences across countries

Although digitalisation is progressing at a steady pace overall for distribution channels, its intensity varies significantly across European countries. For example, regarding the shares of "online first awareness", "only online research" and "online comparison of products" for personal loans, Sweden scores remarkably high, while Belgium and France are consistently very low. France and Belgium still score very high for "only offline research" and "research offline and purchase offline", whereas Estonia, Sweden and the UK reached very low levels. As regards differences across the different phases and countries, the digital market share for "first awareness" is much higher than for the "research of products only online". For instance, the respective market shares reached 88% versus 32% in Germany, 63% versus 15% in Belgium, 75% versus 31% in France and 77% versus 36% in Ireland. This is relevant to information asymmetry. Also, as emphasised in the chapter on the use of alternative data, the share of consumers that share their customer experience on social media varies noticeably from country to country.

Figure 5. Distribution channels for personal loans, by country (2015, % of total)

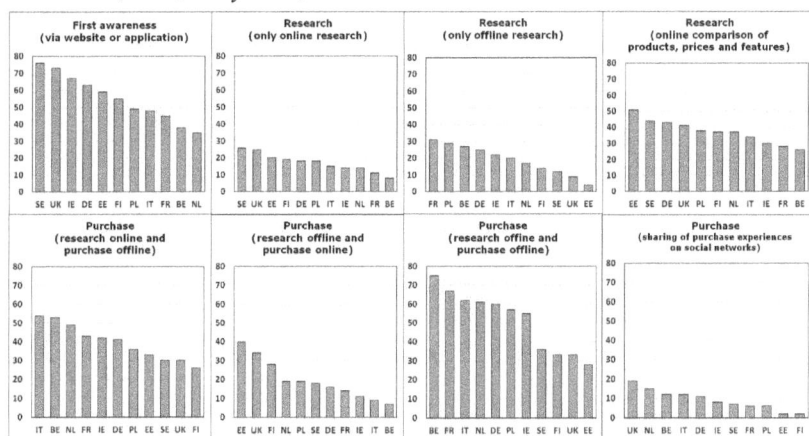

Source: Author based on Google Consumer Barometer Survey (2015).

Different devices involved

Still according to the Google Consumer Barometer Survey (2015), the most important device used for product research on both personal loans and car insurances remains the computer (see below Figure 6): on average 85% of the consumers using online distribution channels for personal loans connected at least once through this device (84.2% for car insurance). Due to the still limited number of alternatives, for car insurance, all countries excluding Belgium, Italy and Finland recorded a share above 80%.

The corresponding unweighted average of smartphone and tablet use for researching personal loans stood at only 19% and 14%, respectively (20.7% and 19.7% for car insurance, respectively). Nevertheless, only a few years ago tablets and mobile devices were absent from personal loan distribution channels. In this context, the growth in the use of these devices has been very pronounced and most likely the related shares will continue to grow at a steady pace in the forthcoming years, especially for smartphones.[24] Interestingly, for most countries, the aggregate figures in percentages by country are all much above 100%, as a result of hybrid consumer behaviour regarding the use of devices. A significant share of consumers use different types of devices during the pre-sale and sales phases.

As regards information disclosure requirements and advertisements, policy-makers need to consider that possibilities vary across these different devices. Different screen sizes, different levels of flexibility, etc., imply that some specific mandatory requirements might make sense for one device but might be inadequate for another.

---

[24] This potential shift from personal computer towards mobile devices to carry out online activities has been identified by many stakeholders in the study conducted by CEPS for DG FISMA (2016) as one of the main drivers of innovation in both the collection of data and their use to improve the efficiency of digital distribution channels, notably through the development of data analytics. In this respect, an increase in mobile connectivity will allow for a better use of data collected via geolocation systems and could help providers know their consumers better when they purchase products, do payments, contract loans, etc. Performing mobile applications will be therefore a crucial instrument for providers of personal loans and car insurance to compete in the coming years.

Figure 6. Devices used for product research on personal loans (2015, % of total)

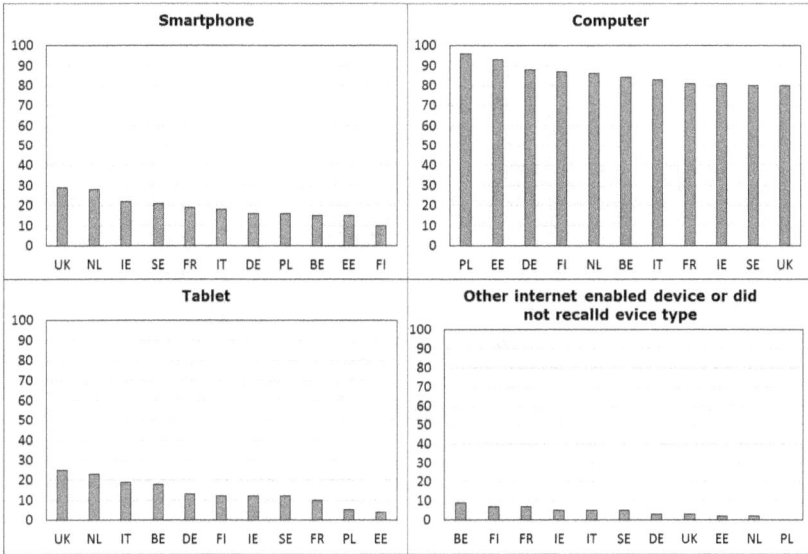

Source: Author based on Google Consumer Barometer Survey (2015).

Figure 7. Devices used for product research on car insurance (2015, in % of total)

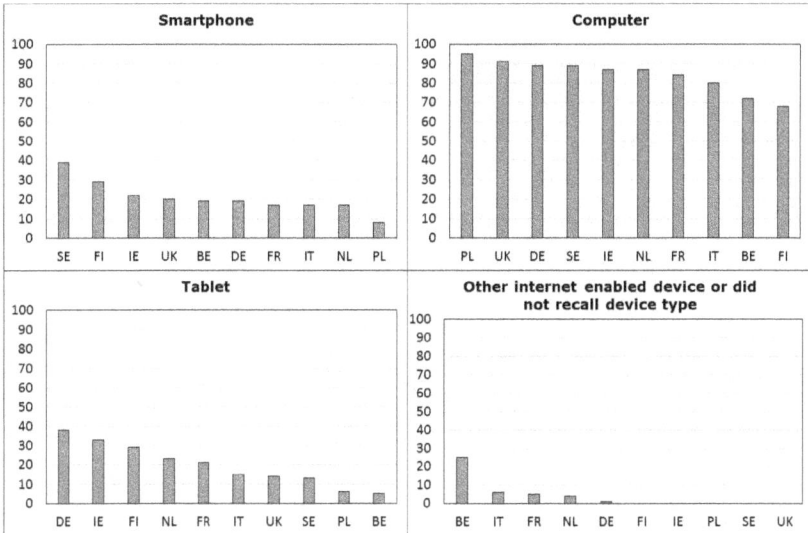

Source: Author based on Google Consumer Barometer Survey (2015).

3.2 Review of online aspects in existing European rules for pre-contractual information duties

General directives

The Connected Digital Single Market agenda enhanced by the European Commission includes the modernisation and simplification of consumer rules for online and digital purchases. Different initiatives have been taken by European institutions to achieve this objective, notably a Fitness Check (Q1 2015-Q2 2017) aimed at exploring the ways to improve the application of current EU legislation and, based on these findings, to determine if there is a need for further legislative action at EU level (see European Commission, 2015a). The Fitness Check focuses on specific general directives on consumer protection, some of them covering advertisement and information disclosure requirements: price indication Directive (European Commission, 1998), unfair commercial practices Directive (European Commission, 2005) and the misleading and comparative advertising Directive (European Commission, 2006a). The more recent consumer rights Directive (European Commission, 2011a) is assessed separately by the Commission. Two other directives that are not covered by this Fitness Check and that also contain consumer information requirements are the e-Commerce Directive (European Commission, 2000) and the services Directive (European Commission, 2006b). The original objectives of each directive can be found in Box 3.

Box 3. Original objectives of general directives on consumer protection

Price indication Directive (1998)

The original objective of this directive is to establish a high level of consumer protection through improved consumer information regarding the indication of the selling price and the price per unit of measurement of products.

Unfair commercial practices Directive (2005)

The original objective of this directive is to establish a high level of consumer protection and reduce obstacles to the Single Market by fully harmonising national laws in the area of consumer protection against unfair commercial practices.

Misleading and comparative advertising Directive (2006a)

The original objective of the directive is to reduce obstacles to the Single Market by approximating national laws protecting traders against misleading advertising and its unfair consequences. This directive places the focus on all business-to-business (B2B) advertising.

Consumer rights Directive (2011a)

The original objective of the directive is to harmonise information disclosure requirements for the purchase of goods or services both on the trader's premises and away from the trader's premises, cancellation rights and responsibilities for goods or services purchased away from the trader's premises, delivery times for goods and fees charged for a particular method, e.g. credit card surcharges.

E-Commerce Directive (2000)

The original objective of the directive is to establish harmonised rules on issues such as the transparency and information requirements for online service providers, commercial communications, electronic contracts and limitations of liability of intermediary service providers.

Services Directive (2006b)

The original objective of the directive is to realise the full potential of services markets in Europe by removing legal and administrative barriers to trade.

Financial services directives

These general directives are the basis of the consumer protection rules in terms of information disclosure and advertisement. Nevertheless, excluding the e-commerce Directive, they do not apply to retail financial services (see Table 2).

Owing to their original characteristics, services sold in retail banking and non-life insurance have been the object of specific directives that also cover information disclosure requirements, which can be online and/or offline, and complement the related requirements of the general directives above (the original objectives of each directive can be found in Box 4). These consist of:

- Directive on distance marketing of consumer financial services (European Commission, 2002)
- Consumer credit Directive (European Commission, 2008, 2011b)
- Mortgage credit Directive (European Commission, 2014a)
- Payment accounts Directive (European Commission, 2014b)
- Payment services Directive 2 (European Commission, 2015b)
- Insurance distribution Directive (European Commission, 2016)

Box 4. Original objectives of financial services directives on consumer protection

Directive on distance marketing of consumer financial services (2002)

The original objective of this directive is to harmonise principles relating to financial services that may be provided at a distance (especially with a supplier established in another member state). The directive notably focuses on the obligation of providers to provide consumers with comprehensive information before a contract is concluded and on the ban of abusive marketing practices (such as 'inertia selling', in which a consumer is sent a product s/he did not ask for and is then sent a follow-up bill).

Consumer credit Directive (2008, 2011b)

The original objective of this directive is to foster the integration of consumer credit markets in the EU and to ensure a high level of consumer protection by focusing on transparency and consumer rights. It stipulates that a comprehensible set of information should be given to consumers in good time, before the contract is concluded and also as part of the credit agreement. In order to allow consumers to compare more easily the various offers and to better understand the information provided, creditors have to provide pre-contractual information in a standardised form. Providers will have to provide consumers with the Annual Percentage Rate of Charge (APR), which is a single figure, harmonised at EU level and representing the total cost of the credit (amendment of the Directive in 2011). In addition, consumers have the right to withdraw within a period of 14 days after the conclusion of the contract and they have the possibility to repay their credit early at any time (against a fair and objectively justified compensation).

Mortgage credit Directive (2014a)

The original objective of this directive is to create a Union-wide mortgage credit market with a focus on consumer information requirements, principle-based rules and standards for the performance of services, a consumer creditworthiness assessment obligation, provisions on early repayment, provisions on foreign currency loans, provision on tying practices, some high-level principles and a passport for credit intermediaries who meet the admission requirements in their home member state.

Payment accounts Directive (2014b)

The original objective of the directive is to enhance access to bank accounts by providing all EU consumers (even for non-residents and irrespective of their financial situation) with a right to open a bank account that allows them to perform essential operations, such as receiving their salary, pensions and allowances or to pay utility bills. Also, the directive aims at making it easier for consumers to compare the fees charged for bank accounts by providers in the EU. Finally, the establishment of a simple and quick procedure for consumers who wish to switch their bank account to one with another provider within the same member state and to assist consumers who hold a bank account and want to open another account in a different country.

Payment services Directive 2 (2015b)

The original objective of the directive is to provide the legal foundation for the creation of an EU-wide single market for payments. It introduces strict security requirements for the initiation and processing of electronic payments and the protection of consumers' financial data. It opens the EU payment market for companies offering consumer or business-oriented payment services based on the access to information about the payment account – the so-called PISP and AISP. It enhances consumers' rights in numerous areas, including reducing the liability for non-authorised payments, introducing an unconditional ('no questions asked') refund right for direct debits in euros and prohibits surcharging (additional charges for the right to pay, e.g. with a card) whether the payment instrument is used in shops or online.

Insurance distribution Directive (2016)

The original objective of the directive is to regulate all distributors of insurance products, including online distributors. The directive specifies the information that should be given to consumers before they sign an insurance contract, imposes certain conduct of business and transparency rules on distributors, clarifies the rules for cross-border business and addresses the supervision and sanctioning of insurance distributors if they breach the provisions of the directive.

The core directive that has structured obligations in terms of pre-contractual information disclosure for online channels is the Directive on distance marketing of retail financial services (DMRFS) in 2002, at a time when online research and purchase of financial services was still in its early stage. Nevertheless, the definition of "distance contracts" was broader than those concluded online and could cover a significant share of the market. Indeed, according to Article 2 of the directive, "distance contract" means any contract concerning financial services concluded between a supplier and a consumer under an organised distance sales or service-provision scheme run by the supplier, who, for the purpose of that contract, makes exclusive use of one or more means of distance communication up to and including the time at which the contract is concluded.

The means of distance communication refers to any means which, without the simultaneous physical presence of the supplier and the consumer, may be used for the distance marketing of a service between those parties: online, telephone, mails, etc. This directive aims at covering all financial services that have a banking, credit, insurance, personal pension, investment or payment nature.

As emphasised in the Point (5) of the directive, because of their intangible nature, financial services are particularly well suited to distance selling, and the establishment of a "legal framework governing the distance marketing of financial services should boost consumer confidence in the use of new techniques for the distance marketing of financial services, such as electronic commerce". In the context of the introduction of the euro as a single currency, the main objective of this directive was to contribute to reinforcing the single market for these financial services. The key assumption was that, as the respective locations of consumers and providers matter little in the context of distance contracts, a harmonised regulatory framework should result in further cross-border sales, thereby strengthening the single market.

However, as highlighted in the Commission's Communication COM(2009) 626 (European Commission, 2009), the market for distance selling of financial services had not changed significantly since the introduction of the directive, and the market share of cross-border sales remained very low despite increasing internet penetration among households.

Even though the policy objective of reinforcing the single market was not achieved, this directive has remained the cornerstone for all directives that have been enacted since then and that have set rules on the pre-contractual information to be provided to consumers for distance contracts. In 2008, the consumer credit Directive (CCD) established the detailed list of standardised information to be provided specifically for consumer credit (within the Standard European Consumer Credit Information, SECCI), but no adjustments were made regarding the core process of disclosure for distance contracts. As regards the mortgage credit Directive (MCD) of 2014, in line with the CCD, a very detailed list of information to be disclosed was defined (within the European Standardised Information Sheet, ESIS) and some elements supplemented the DMRFS for the distance mortgage contracts. Notably, given the significance of the financial commitment for the consumer, the supplier has to provide pre-contractual information before the mortgage credit agreement.

The payment accounts Directive (2014) introduced specific new elements regarding information disclosure with distance payment account contracts. Given that the share of payment accounts purchased online is significantly higher than for household loans, the directive emphasises further the process to follow for information disclosure. According to Article 4(5), the fee information document and the glossary shall be made available to consumers at any time by payment service providers. They shall be provided in an easily manner, including to non-customers, in electronic format on their websites, where available, and in the premises of payment service providers accessible to consumers. One original element in that directive is that suppliers have to provide document on paper or another durable medium free of charge only at the request by a consumer.

Another original element in that directive is the objective of regulating comparison websites: according to Article 7, member states shall ensure that consumers have access, free of charge, to a least one website comparing fees charged by payment service providers for at least the services listed in the directive. This article sets the rules to which these comparative websites need to comply, including a detailed list of information that must be disclosed to consumers on the characteristics of the website.

In its Articles 44 through 58, the payment services Directive (PSD2) establishes a long list of information to be disclosed for each specific situation of payment (contract agreement, transaction, consumer, merchants, etc.) that also covers remote payment contract and transaction. In Article 39, the PSD2 clearly indicates that specific articles on mandatory information disclosure replace some articles in the DMRFS in order to be more in line with current trends.

Finally, the insurance distribution Directive supplies a detailed list of conditions and means through which the mandatory information has to be disclosed. Provided that consumers have been given the choice between information on paper, durable media, and websites and that the provision of information using one specific means is regarded as appropriate in the context of the business conducted between the insurance distributor and the consumer, any of these means can be used (some further conditions are required for each means).

Overall, despite the fact that the core Directive on distance contracts for financial services was enacted in 2002, when digital technologies were still in an early stage of development, subsequent directives on types of financial services have not or have scarcely departed from the core rules of the Directive regarding pre-contractual information duties. Within the context of increasing disruption by enabling financial technologies and continuously higher market shares of financial services sold online, an adjustment will be needed in the coming years.

Table 2. Specific requirements for the online/offline information disclosure in European rules

Regulation	Year	New specific require-ments for the online info disclosure	Applies to consumer financial services	Details
General directives				
Price indication Directive	1998	No		
e-commerce Directive	2000	Yes	Yes	
Unfair commercial practices Directive	2005		No[25]	Point (18): Development of the benchmark of 'average consumer' and 'vulnerable consumer'
Services Directive	2006		No[26]	
Misleading & comparative advertising Directive	2006		No[27]	
Consumer rights Directive	2011		No[28]	
Directives for retail banking and non-life insurance				
Directive on distance marketing of consumer financial	2002	Yes	Yes (incl. insurance)	Art. 2: definition of "distance contract" is not limited to online contracts Art. 3: detailed list of information to provide to consumer prior to

---

[25] This directive provides for full harmonisation of the respective rules across the EU with the exception of financial services and immovable property.

[26] See Article 2, 2b.

[27] This directive applies to all business-to-business (B2B) advertising.

[28] See Article 3, 3d.

services (DMRFS)				the conclusion of the distance contract Art. 5: -Point (1) The supplier shall communicate mandatory pre-contractual information on paper or on another durable medium available & accessible to the consumer in good time before the consumer is bound by any distance contract or offer -Point (2) The supplier shall fulfil his obligation under above paragraph 1 immediately after the conclusion of the contract, if the contract has been concluded at the consumer's request using a means of distance communication which does not enable providing the contractual terms & conditions, and the information in conformity with paragraph 1
Consumer credit Directive	2008 -11	No (in line with DMRFS)	Yes	Article 5: in case of use of distance communication, pre-contractual information of the SECCI immediately after the contract at the latest ANNEX II: Additional information in the case of distance contracts
Mortgage credit Directive	2014		Yes	(21): Supplement the (DMRFS) for distance mortgage contracts: pre-contractual information on the right of withdrawal has to be provided before the conclusion of the contract Art. 14: to conform to the DMRFS, the ESIS has to be provided prior to the conclusion of the contract ANNEX II, B, Point (3): specific elements on the ESIS in case of distance contracts (in line with DMRFS)
Payment accounts Directive	2014		Yes	Art. 4: The fee information document shall be:

				-made available to consumers at any time by payment service providers -provided in an easily accessible manner in electronic format on their websites where available and in the premises of payment service providers accessible to consumers, as well as on paper or another durable medium free of charge upon request by a consumer Art. 7: focus on comparison websites: obligation to have at least one independent website (free of charge) comparing fees charged by payment service providers for specific services; specific information on the website needs to be disclosed
Payment services Directive 2	2015		Yes	Art. 4: notion of "remote payment transaction": a payment transaction initiated via Internet or through a device that can be used for distance communication Arts 44 through 58: detailed list of information to be provided to the payment service user for each specific situation Art. 51: conclusion of a distance contract: pre-contractual information to be provided at the latest immediately after the framework contract Art. 39: for distant contracts, information requirements in Art. 3(1) of DMRFS – excluding points (2)(c) through (g), (3)(a), (d) and (e), and (4)(b) – shall be replaced by Arts 44, 45, 51 and 52 of PSD2

Insurance Distribution	2016		Yes	Art. 23: information conditions for the providence of information -Point (1): clear/accurate/comprehensible; by default on paper; free of charge; language of MS where risk is situated or MS of the commitment/any other language agreed upon by the parties -Points (2) through (7): detailed list of conditions to provide the information on media other than paper

Source: Author.

3.3 Need for consistency of rules across distribution channels

Observations of trends in section 3.1 show that:

- The online market share for research of financial services is today very significant.

- The omnichannel model where consumers combine both online and offline channels to search and purchase a product is also significant.

- The pace of digitalisation of distribution channels varies markedly across countries.

- New online devices such as smartphones and tablets are entering the market and already cover a significant share of the research process in some countries.

These trends will need to be further addressed in future European rules on distance sales of financial services. The growing popularity of the omnichannel approach raises issues regarding the consistency of rules across online and offline channels. The principle of non-discrimination across both types of channels has been the key driver behind successive European rules on pre-contractual information duties of financial service providers. Regardless of the means through which the information is supplied to consumers (paper, any durable medium or website), the type of standardised information and the timing are similar across both channels.

Nevertheless, with the multiplication of devices that shape the interactions between suppliers and consumers, the principle of non-discrimination will likely require further legislative elements. For instance, increasing numbers of consumers use mobile telephones in their search for products, often with small screens that have restrictions on the number of characters and this element has not been covered yet in directives on financial services.

It is worth noting that, in its Point (36), the consumer rights Directive (2011) establishes that the information requirements should be adapted to take into account the technical constraints of the type of media (mobile telephone screens, SMS, television sales spots, etc.). In such cases, the trader should comply with a minimum set of information requirements and refer the consumer to another source of information, for instance by providing a toll free telephone number or hypertext link to the webpage of the trader where the relevant information is directly available and easily accessible.[29] Nevertheless, this directive does not apply to financial services, although, due to their complexity, much information is required for these types of product.

Also, a key aspect concerns the differentiated pace of digitalisation across countries (see Figure 4 above). European and national policy-makers should develop tools that promote convergence in the digitalisation of distribution channels across Europe. Such convergence can help reinforce the single market, thereby contributing to further choices and competition.

---

[29] More specifically, Article 8(4) provides the minimum set of pre-contractual information to be provided for contracts concluded using technologies such as SMS, which impose technical limits on the amount of information that can be sent. It also identifies the information that should be provided if the trader has customised the content and presentation of his trading website for mobile devices with small screens. In these cases, the trader can limit the information displayed on the user's screen to that required under Article 8(4), where appropriate in an expandable format, without obliging the consumer to navigate away from the page being used to place the order. The rest of the pre-contractual information required under Article 6(1) could in this case be available via hyperlink (see also recital 36, which refers to "providing a toll free telephone number or a hypertext link to a webpage" in the case of distance contracts concluded through means of distance communication with technical constraints).

3.4 Role of behavioural insights and big data analytics: 'Standardised' versus 'personalised' disclosed information

Emergence of behavioural insights in recent years

Behavioural economics has become increasingly popular over the last decade. Some domestic regulatory bodies, such as the Financial Conduct Authority (FCA) in the UK and the Netherlands Authority for the Financial Markets (AFM), are vigorously promoting possibilities for applying behavioural insights to financial regulations.

This approach aims at analysing and correcting specific market dysfunctions that can be sparked by behavioural biases of consumers. The core assumption is that consumers do not systematically choose their products in their best interests, as their behaviour and purchasing strategies are markedly influenced by specific context and psychological factors. More specifically, three cognitive limits may induce the violation of rational assumptions (Jolls et al., 2000):

(1) Bounded rationality: limits faced by human beings in terms of accessible information, mental capacity and available time (Simon, 1957).

(2) Bounded willpower: people act in conflict with their long-term interest, even though they anticipate negative effects in so doing, e.g. smoking, over-spending today instead of saving for old age (de Manuel et al., 2014).

(3) Bounded self-interest: people care about treating others fairly because they want to be treated in the same way: agents will act 'nicer' or 'nastier' depending on how the other party treats them.

Over-reliance on standardised information disclosure policy of European rules

European directives shaping consumer protection rules for all types of retail financial services have heavily relied on standardised pre-contractual information duties policies, in particular the consumer credit Directive and the mortgage credit Directive. Standardised disclosure policy is typically at the base of many consumer policies because:

- it is often less controversial and complicated to implement (such as suitability requirements or restrictions on product features);

- in principle, harmonised terminology and standards should contribute to reducing the administrative costs of bringing new products to new markets; and

- theoretically, it alleviates search costs for consumers.

However, the implementation of harmonised disclosure contains several significant pitfalls:

- The very long and detailed lists of mandatory information to be disclosed according to some European rules make the whole process relatively burdensome for banks (in addition, each country has the possibility to add other types of mandatory information to be disclosed).

- Due to their 'bounded rationality' emphasised above, many consumers do not read this large amount of information, read it superficially or read it in details but partially understand the implications (such as the true meaning of the standardised annual percentage rate: see, for example, Raynard, 2014).

While the regulatory options to alleviate the negative effects of the 'bounded willpower' or 'bounded self-interest' appear to be relatively limited, policy-makers should have further possibilities to lessen the negative effects of 'bounded rationality'. Analyses of specific behavioural biases that contribute to bounded rationality help us to better understand what is at stake and to enhance corrective measures.

Emergence of big data analytics

As revealed in Figure 2 in chapter 2, owing to the very marked growth in the volume of digital personal data stored in recent years, a particular big data activity is rapidly emerging. An increasing number of financial suppliers are integrating complex algorithms based on big data analytics and machine learning that process vast amounts of personal data, thereby contributing to disrupting traditional business models. This growing popularity for big data analytics could also significantly disrupt the regulatory approach towards standardised information disclosure.

Possibility to develop a new policy model of 'smart disclosure duties'

Technically, providers that already use big data analytics and behavioural insights in order to develop increasingly refined segmentation for marketing, creditworthiness, insurance pricing, prevention, etc., should also be able to create a segmentation of the consumers according to what type of information they might need in order to make their choices in adequate conditions. Examples of what could be personalised information disclosure include elements from both the content of this information and the way this information is presented.

In the online world, where people are bombarded with more and more information, understanding where attention and focus are attracted can help in the design of more effective communication. Some research, such as in Benartzi (2015), is increasingly focusing on online behaviour and the impact of specific types of messages. Possibilities in terms of 'framing'[30] are much broader online than offline and could be personalised for each consumer, based on which option carries the most impact for each. For instance, a segmentation that distinguishes consumers who have already missed payments in the last three years from those who have not could help suppliers disclose information in a more personal way: through the use of colours, specific fonts or even other tools such as videos, popups or digital pictures, specific information could be further emphasised for consumers with past missed payments.

Such a model can help maintain an adequate balance between consumers and suppliers regarding the information asymmetries analysed in the previous chapter on alternative data. To a certain

---

[30] 'Positive framing' concerns a practice by which the information or choices are presented in a way that accentuates positive aspects of the consequences or outcomes. Whether a choice is framed in a positive or negative way can have a huge impact on how people evaluate the choice. For instance, framing the future in a positive way can motivate people to work hard to attain the positive outcome.

extent, it could better match the growing role of robo-advisers and the gradual disappearance of call centres or face-to-face interactions in branches. Provided that they have sufficient amounts of personal data on consumers who gave consent to share it, suppliers that use big data analytics could personalise not only their marketing campaigns, but also pre-contractual information disclosure and help consumers better understand the products available.

Main regulatory challenges to the development of the new policy model of 'smart disclosure'

Task Force members emphasised specific challenges that have to be addressed to develop this new policy model of 'smart disclosure'.

1.   Voluntary basis

As emphasised in Busch (2016), the development of such a model can only result from the choice of both the supplier and the consumer:

-    only finance service providers that use big data analytics to a significant extent can implement the needed processes; and
-    in line with the general data protection Regulation (2016), the collection of the needed personal data requires the consent of the consumer.

As a consequence, depending on the decision of the consumer, there will be two possibilities:

-    if the consumer does not give his consent to use his personal data, he will receive standardised pre-contractual data; or
-    if the consumer agrees with sharing his personal data, then he will receive personalised data that should better assist him in the choice of the most appropriate financial product.

2.   Review or continuation of some core concepts of the existing European rules

Some of the core elements of the conceptual framework that has shaped the European policy-making process for consumer protection should be challenged by this new model. For example, as highlighted in the unfair commercial practices Directive (2005), two types of consumers are benchmarked in order to assess the impact of commercial practice: the 'average' consumer and the 'vulnerable' consumer. The former is reasonably well-informed, observant and circumspect, whereas the latter has characteristics that make him or her more vulnerable to unfair commercial practices.

The directive establishes that pools of vulnerable consumers have to be assessed via the average consumer of each pool. In a context of widespread use of big data analytics and behavioural insights that personalise information disclosure, the very notion of 'benchmark consumer' could become obsolete, because much better knowledge of each consumer should help design personalised information disclosure that adequately addresses the needs of each specific consumer.

On the other hand, some European legal concepts should be maintained in order to ensure overall legal consistency, at least in the initial stages of implementation. For example, the provision of advisory services is not compulsory within European legislation and such obligation may be decided only by member states for specific situations (see for instance the mortgage credit Directive, 2014).[31] One risk is that the development of pre-contractual personalised information duties might overlap somehow with the obligation to advise, given that within this model some pieces of information might be further emphasised depending on the consumer's profile. Nevertheless, in order to maintain a balance between the responsibilities and rights of both consumers and providers, a clear distinction still needs to be made between information disclosure and advice. Should a consumer have further questions about a product and not be satisfied with the information disclosed, the provider still has the obligation to inform this consumer about the existence of advisory services, if any.

---

[31] See for example Article 22 of the mortgage credit Directive (2014), which obliges the creditor, credit intermediary or appointed representative to explicitly inform the consumer, in the context of a given transaction, whether advisory services are being or can be provided to the consumer. Member states may provide for an obligation for the provider or the intermediary to warn a consumer when, considering the consumer's financial situation, a credit agreement may induce a specific risk for the consumer (see European Commission, 2014a).

3. *Difficulty in enforcing the new rules*

Obviously, monitoring compliance with personalised information duties is more complex than with standardised information (Busch, 2016). In theory, regulators should ensure that the algorithm used for generating consumer information has the right granularity. One possibility for the supervisors will be to assess whether the segmentation developed for marketing and information disclosure purposes has broadly the same level of granularity.

4. *Risk of 'over-disclosure'*

One of the core original objectives of smart disclosure is to create a less burdensome process for both suppliers and consumers. If some conditions are not be fulfilled, there are significant risks that this objective might not be achieved and that the whole process might even result in 'over-disclosure'. For instance, the consumer's consent regarding the use of his or her personal data will be confirmed through a 'privacy statement', which should provide information on how their data will be processed, on their rights to know when their data has been hacked, etc. (in line with the GDPR requirements).

Furthermore, regarding the content of the disclosed pre-contractual information, one of the possible risks of the use of a high-granularity algorithm could be 'hyper information', whereby suppliers provide very detailed information on each consumer. In this context, the bounded rationality of consumers would be even further tested and the final outcome counterproductive.

Against this background, the development of a 'smart disclosure' regulation needs to clearly emphasise that the purpose is simplification. One possibility would be to have a shorter list of mandatory information that suppliers have to disclose. For the rest, it will depend on the findings resulting from the developed segmentation.

5. *Complexity of products*

One of the reasons highlighted by regulators for designing rules with a large amount of mandatory information to disclose is to help consumers cope with the ever increasing complexity of products, especially in some domestic markets. One resulting argument would be that simplification of the disclosed information would weaken the ability of consumers to truly understand what is at stake. However, as analysed above, limited rationality of consumers implies that this information is not adequately processed by a significant share of consumers, if not the vast majority. Therefore, an appropriate balance between the level of complexity of the product and the quality/quantity of the disclosed information needs to be defined by suppliers, consumers and regulators.

6.   Risk of data discrimination

Finally, the algorithm aimed at segmenting consumers for the disclosed information needs to be highly reliable. In case of misinterpretation of the 'information needs' of different groups of consumers, the disclosed information could be optimal for some groups of consumers and suboptimal for others. These dysfunctions could be interpreted as 'data discrimination', because some consumers would have to decide when lacking information they truly need while some other consumers will have this information.

Beyond the reliability of the developed processes, such a new philosophy could be the opportunity to promote a shared responsibility between consumers and suppliers. First, a system could be developed whereby consumers are given the choice to assess their ability to read and understand pre-contractual information. This system will include questions with multiple choice answers, e.g. "Do you consider your understanding of financial information is: very poor, poor, average, high or very high?" For each answer, an adequate set of information and layout will be provided. This system might be less advantageous for consumers, as the burden of choice and subsequent outcomes should fall predominantly on the customer. In order to address this issue, the assessment of the consumer's financial knowledge could result from some combination of self-assessment and provider assessment (which could also include the submission of several questions to the consumer).

4. HOW TO IMPROVE THE REGULATORY FRAMEWORK FOR DIGITAL AUTHENTICATION?

The success of the digital transformation of retail banking and non-life insurance significantly depends on the ability of the sector to develop robust remote authentication processes. One of the objectives of the EU is to render strong digital authentication between the different stakeholders not only within countries but also across countries. In that context, the main aim of the recently enacted eIDAS Regulation (European Commission, 2014b) is to ensure the proper functioning of the internal market, and grant appropriate security level and legal certainty on the electronic interaction across member states.

The purpose of this chapter is to identify through which channels and to what extent the implementation of the eIDAS could benefit retail banking and non-life insurance. Next, remaining regulatory issues and challenges regarding the application of the eIDAS and its consistency with typical financial rules such as the PSD2 Directive (2015) and the anti-money laundering (AML) Directive (European Commission, 2015c) are assessed. Finally, we analyse some additional issues that are not directly addressed by the eIDAS.

Recommendations

1. Gradually assessing the possibilities and challenges to extend the e-IDAS to the private sector.

2. Reinforcing consistency between e-IDAS and domestic AML rules.

3. Assessing the obstacles to the remote identification of non-resident consumers of retail financial services.

4. Continuously ensuring that the regulatory approach of the e-IDAS is adaptable to the pace of technological change.

5. Systematically removing discrimination against reliance on third parties.

4.1   Introduction to eIDAS

The eIDAS is the first significant step towards a complete digital single market for electronic identification signature and other trust services. The new legal framework constituted by this Regulation and the implementing acts issued by the Commission introduce specific legal and technical provisions in terms of issuance and mutual recognition of the electronic identification and trust services. The grounding principle constituting the backbone of the Regulation is twofold: i) providing full cross-border mutual recognition and ii) ensuring equal legal effectiveness of both traditional and digital means.

To be effective, the means of national electronic identification (eID) has to be issued in compliance with the list published by the European Commission on European electronic identification schemes, and it must guarantee adequate assurance level and security standards. Between 29 September 2015 and 29 September 2018, member states may voluntarily notify and recognise the electronic ID. Thereafter, mutual recognition of notified eIDs will be mandatory.

Table 3 below summarises the structure of eID systems in some EU countries. According to their national eID schemes, which are defined by national law, a member state's citizens have access to different eID means. For public eID means, the government is responsible for the production, distribution and maintenance of the data and devices related to the issued eID. For private eID means the issuing party is a private company, certified and supervised by the government, responsible for the production and maintenance of the eID. In some countries, private and public means coexist. Where available, the eID means are conceived for both public and private use, namely e-government and e-business.

The fourth column provides the information on the eID means available to the customer for access to e-government services in the selected countries. Where applicable, the fifth column reports the eID means available at present for e-banking services in the selected countries.

Table 3. Type of eID mean, e-service, e-government and e-banking, by country

Country	eID mean	Type of eService	eGovernment	eBanking
Austria	Public eID	Public and Private use	Public eID	eBanking STORK 2 Pilot Project with Public eID (ongoing)
Belgium	Public eID	Public and Private use	Public eID	No
Denmark	Private eID mean (NemID) under the control of the state	Public and Private use	NemID	Yes
Estonia	Public and Private eID means	Public and Private use	Public and Private eID (interoperable)	Public and Private eID (interoperable)
France	Not available	No	Username and password (provided by each service provider)	No
Germany	Public eID	Public and Private use	Public eID	No
Ireland	Not available	No	PPSN (Personal Public Service Number) and Secure PIN (provided by the service provider)	PPSN and Secure PIN (available for Income Tax only)
Italy	Private eID means under the control of the state	Public and Private use	SPID (Public System for Digital Identity)	No
Netherlands	Public and Private eID means	Public and Private use	Idensys, DigiD	iDEAL, iDIN

Spain	Public eID (DNIe) and private means	Public and Private use	DNIe, Digital Certificate from CERES (Public Certification Authority)	No
Sweden	Public and Private eID means	Public and Private use	Public and Private eID means	Private eID means (mainly BankID)
United Kingdom	Private eID mean	Public and Private use	Private eID means thought the platform Gov.Uk Verify	Yes

Source: European Commission and author.

4.2 Opportunities of the eIDAS

Opportunity 1: Core guidelines for the digital transformation

Provisions on eIDs under eIDAS are mandatory for e-government, but each member state is free to extend their eID systems to the private sector. In this context, the eIDAS is likely to have little direct impact on retail financial services. Nevertheless, the framework developed in the Regulation that aims at ensuring mutual recognition of all the notified eID schemes in Europe in the public sector could serve as basic guidelines for retail banks that are digitalising all of their interactions with consumers. Once customers have passed anti-money laundering verifications (AML identification) and can be granted trusted identity status (see Figure 8 below), they will be able to conduct all of their banking activities digitally.

Figure 8. Opening a (current) account: What are the relevant requirements?

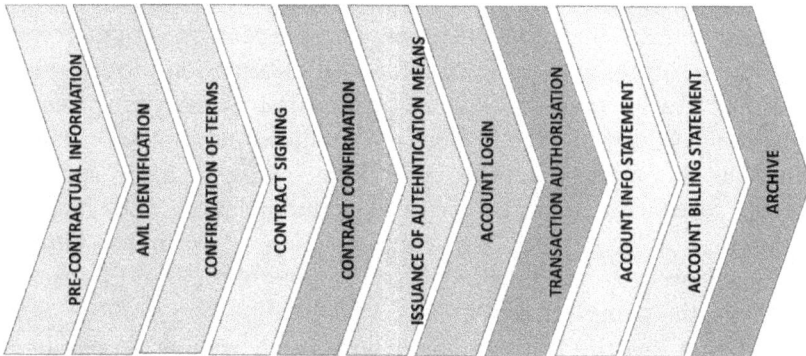

Source: Author based on Linde (2016).

Due to its broad scope, the eIDAS should also help clarify how the financial sector will be able to comply with some key rules of ambitious financial legislations, such as PSD2. For instance, on the draft Regulatory Technical Standards specifying the requirements on strong customer authentication and common and secure communication under PSD2 (EBA, 2016), the EBA states in Article 20 that for the purpose of identification, payment service providers (PSP) shall rely on qualified certificates for website authentication as per Article 3(39) of the eIDAS.

Opportunity 2: Consistency across the different channels

In certain countries, one of the main obstacles to the full digitalisation of distribution channels in retail banking and non-life insurance is that only paper-based signatures can complete a contract. One of the main consequences of the eIDAS is that there will be no more discrimination between paper and online signature. In particular, the new legal framework on e-signature solves the current problem of handwritten signatures on digitalised documents often having no legal value.

Opportunity 3: Cost efficiency for suppliers

E-signatures as defined and shaped in the eIDAS will help organisations save paper, storage space, time (for, e.g. scanning), postal costs, resources for non-repudiation in electronically fulfilled transactions, etc.

Opportunity 4: More access and trust for consumers

In theory, within such a framework, companies could develop models where no face-to-face interactions are required anymore. As shown in Figures 3 and 4 in chapter 3 on information disclosure in a digital era, the pre-contractual phase (first awareness, research and comparison) is already highly digitalised, while the purchase phase is still largely conducted offline, owing to the respective needs for face-to-face advice and authentication and manual signatures to complete the contract. Regarding more simple financial products such as current accounts, eIDAS could quickly facilitate the complete digitalisation of the distribution chain. The popularity of the omnichannel approach, where consumers combine both online and offline channels, could gradually lessen and the remote access and digital malleability for consumers will increase significantly, provided that strong digital on-boarding platforms are developed.

Therefore, retail banks and non-life insurance could more adequately respond to the increasing digital expectations of consumers who have high digital literacy (especially younger generations). As regards consumers who have lower digital literacy and are often more risk averse, their trust in digital tools for purchasing financial products could increase thanks to rules that are fit to cope with cybercrimes, enhance the possibility of using a specific number of electronic identification means and aim at shaping the environment for trusting service providers.

Opportunity 5: Delivering trust for the single market

Delivering trust is even more important in the case of cross-border interactions, which is the original objective of the eIDAS. Prior to the eIDAS, the 1999 Directive did not ensure the interoperability and acceptance of electronic signatures across member states. One of the core novelties of the eIDAS is to design a comprehensive mutually acceptable and directly applicable framework aimed at allowing smoother cross-sector interoperability.

EIDAS is expected to enhance the perceived sense of (legal) certainty for consumers who go digital on a cross-border basis, as electronic identification schemes must specify their assurance levels, ranging between low, substantial and/or high. The obligation to recognise electronic identification means should relate only to those consumers who have corresponding levels that are equal or that are higher than the online service in question. The new regulation specifies that member states have the freedom to accept or decline electronic identification means with lower identity assurance levels, which almost certainly helps increase consumer trust.

4.3   Challenges ahead

Challenge 1: eIDAS limited to government sector

Should the eIDAS be adequately implemented, the direct impact of the new rules on retail banking and non-life insurance should be limited, because its primary focus concerns online public services. Thanks to the eIDAS, when offering cross-border services, member states will have to recognise eID schemes notified under the regulation in another member state, but the private sector is indeed under no such obligation.

According to Point (13) of this Regulation, member states should be able to decide whether to involve the private sector in the provision related to electronic identification for accessing online services. More specifically, Point (17) states that member states should encourage the private sector to voluntarily use electronic identification means under a notified scheme for identification purposes when needed for online service or electronic transactions.

Nevertheless, there is no guarantee that member states will go in that direction. Complete interoperability for public services in line with the eIDAS will have rather limited direct impact on consumers using online banking and insurance services. This can, for example, facilitate the income tax declaration when deductibility can be granted for specific products (payment of mortgage interest rates, health insurance premiums, etc.) or specific products need to be taxed (such as some saving products, etc.). Indirectly, however, the conceptual framework of the eIDAS could help financial suppliers shape the complete digitalisation of their authentication of consumers, both within and between countries.

Challenge 2: Inconsistency between domestic AML rules and eIDAS

Another key challenge concerns the lack of consistency between eIDAS and some domestic rules in terms of anti-money laundering. Despite the recent Fourth European anti-money laundering Directive (May 2015), some national provisions may still oblige financial institutions to physically identify the customer in order to meet the legal requirements established by customer due diligence and anti-money laundering legislation.

For payments and transfers, digital authentication allows a credit institution to verify remotely the customer's identity. However, in some member states, procedures such as opening or closing a current account still require face-to-face interaction between the client and the credit institution (the customer needs to make an appointment with the local branch and bring the required documentation). Some credit institutions in the UK, Germany, Denmark and Estonia allow a customer to open a current account remotely through a digital verification of customer identity, using eID or a webcam. These systems simultaneously reduce administrative costs and increase security standards. Indeed, for each procedure high-resolution video is created and stored with all the valuable information it may contain, such as the customer's voice.

To conclude, ensuring the interoperability of eID schemes and alignment of eIDAS provisions and anti-money laundering measures has to be followed by effective enforcement at the national level.

Challenge 3: Many difficulties in identifying non-resident consumers of retail financial services on a remote basis

Remote identification of the customer's identity in the case of retail financial services is generally possible only for residents in the country in question. By contrast, credit institutions cannot verify remotely the identity of a foreign customer. This limitation decreases competition within the EU retail financial sector and affects EU customer access to the retail financial sector in the single market.

Policy-makers should identify the obstacles to remote identification of non-residents for retail financial services. For example, one of the main barriers concerns the accessibility to relevant information: typically, external data that is needed by banks and insurers to identify customers is available in the registers at the national level only. The development of a reliable and independent European external database with the needed information for anti-fraud purposes and verifying customer identity could be a solution to overcome this specific barrier.

Challenge 4: Regulatory approach that is adaptable to the pace of technological change

Authentication tools are heavy on technological content and thus heavily dependent on the latest technological innovations. For instance, per Table 4 below, there is already great diversity in authentication mechanisms for e-finance and e-payment services. Therefore, it is inherently defensible that this regulation should adopt an approach which is, in the first place, adaptable to the pace of technological change.

Table 4. Authentication mechanisms used in e-finance and e-payment services

Password/PIN	Virtual keyboards
	Partial password
Biometrics	Behavioural biometry
	Keystroke dynamics
	Handwritten signature
	Fingerprint recognition
	Voice recognition
	Facial recognition
	Hand geometry
One Time Password	TAN code list
	Coordinates cards
	Mobile SMS-based
	Token device
	QR codes
eSignature	Local/Computer store of key
	Devise Stored key
	- Memory token (USB)

	- Chip card token (eID)
	- Mobile Phone
Device Authentication	Device registration
	Mobile eBanking application

Note: The list is non-exhaustive.
Source: Author.

As highlighted in Point (26), due to the pace of technological change, the purpose of the eIDAS is indeed to adopt an approach which is open to innovation. In Article 12(3)(a), it is clearly stated that the eIDAS aims to be technology neutral and does not discriminate between any specific national technical solutions for electronic identification within a member state. Interestingly, Article 32(1) states that a qualified preservation service for qualified electronic signatures may be provided only by a qualified trust service provider that uses procedures and technologies capable of extending the trustworthiness of the qualified electronic signature beyond the technological validity period.

Point (61) emphasises that this regulation should ensure the long-term preservation of information, in order to ensure the legal validity of electronic signatures over extended periods of time and guarantee that they can be validated irrespective of future technological changes. Nevertheless, should completely new technologies emerge rapidly (such as blockchain for remote KYC processes), the core legal framework of the eIDAS could be challenged.

According to Article 49, the Commission shall review the application of this regulation by evaluating in particular whether it is appropriate to modify the scope of this regulation or its specific provisions, taking into account the experience gained in its application, as well as technological, market and legal developments. However, the deadline for this Review is 1 July 2020, namely six years after the vote on the regulation. Given the current pace of technological change, a review or at least a follow-up should occur sooner, especially if the aim is to assess whether the scope of the eIDAS could be extended to other sectors, such as retail banking and non-life insurance, where innovative FinTech solutions increasingly affect the contractual phase of products and remote

KYC processes. Based on previous experiences, technology indeed changes rapidly and often leaves regulation outdated.

Challenge 5: Systematically removing discrimination against reliance on third parties

Overall, there are two ways to identify customers remotely:

- directly by technical remote identification means, or
- reliance on another party (often a bank) that has already identified the customer.

The objective of the e-IDAS is to focus on the first possibility and will require some years to harmonise throughout the EU. The core principle of the second possibility is that if one financial organisation in the EU has already identified a consumer and will confirm the data for a second financial organisation, then the second financial organisation should be able to rely on that data. This possibility can be used extensively within specific distribution models with intensive intermediation: brokers, etc. Digitalisation is likely to result in further complex digital distribution chains including several intermediaries, thereby resulting in further needs for the second possibility.

Point (35) of the Fourth anti-money laundering Directive emphasises this possibility (European Commission, 2015c):

> In order to avoid repeated customer identification procedures, leading to delays and inefficiency in business, it is appropriate, subject to suitable safeguards, to allow customers whose identification has been carried out elsewhere to be introduced to the obliged entities.

Nevertheless, in reality many domestic regulators discriminate against reliance on a third party. In France, for instance, this is by default a 'high risk' identification case, triggering difficult mitigating measures in enhanced due diligence. In Germany, this method is almost entirely ruled out due to an opinion by Germany's Federal Financial Supervisory Authority (BaFin), which allows reliance on a third party only within the first 18 months of a new customer identification, leading to the absurd consequence that financial organisations cannot confirm the data of long-term customers for other financial organisations.

The development of the fifth AML Directive is a good opportunity to reassess further that:

- financial organisations can rely on other financial organisations for identification (especially in cases where the identified consumer has an ongoing business relationship with the financial organisation and regardless of the question of when the financial organisation identified that consumer);

- the regulation of identification through a third party should promote risk-based mitigation measures, and should not discriminate against this type of identification by putting it by default in the enhanced due diligence/high-risk AML category.

REFERENCES

AFM-DNB (2016), "More room for innovation in the financial sector: Options for market access, authorisations and supervision", AFM-DNB discussion document, 9 June, pp. 14-15 (www.dnb.nl/en/binaries/Discussion%20 document%20AFM-DNB%20More%20room%20for%20innovation%20in %20the%20financial%20sector_tcm47-345198.pdf).

Arneson, R. (2002, revised 2015), "Equality of Opportunity", in E.N. Zalta (ed.), *The Stanford Encyclopedia of Philosophy* (Summer 2015 Edition) (online) (https://plato.stanford.edu/archives/sum2015/entries/equal-opportunity).

Australian Securities and Investments Commission (ASIC) (2016), "16-185MR ASIC consults on a regulatory sandbox licensing exemption", Press Release, 8 June (http://asic.gov.au/about-asic/media-centre/find-a-media-release/2016-releases/16-185mr-asic-consults-on-a-regulatory-sandbox-licensing-exemption/).

Benartzi, S. (2015), *The Smarter Screen: Surprising Ways to Influence and Improve Online Behavior*, New York, NY: Penguin Random House.

Bouyon, S. et al. (2016), "Study on the role of digitalisation and innovation in creating a true single market for retail financial services and insurance", CEPS, Brussels, 7 December (www.ceps.eu/publications/study-role-digitalisation-and-innovation-creating-true-single-market-retail-financial).

Busch, C. (2015), *The Future of Pre-Contractual Information Duties: From Behavioural Insights to Big Data"*, *Research Handbook on EU Consumer and Contract Law*, Cheltenham: Edward Elgar Publishing, 27 November (https://papers.ssrn.com/sol3/papers.cfm?abstract_id=2728315).

Dahl, D., A.P. Meyer and M.C. Neely (2016), "Scale Matters: Community Banks and Compliance Costs", *The Regional Economist*, July, Federal Reserve Bank of St. Louis (www.stlouisfed.org/publications/regional-economist/july-2016/scale-matters-community-banks-and-compliance-costs).

de Galhau, F.V. (2016), "Les banques et les assurances face à la révolution digitale", Speech at ACPR Conference, 25 November (www.banque-france.fr/intervention/les-banques-et-les-assurances-face-la-revolution-digitale).

De Nederlandsche Bank (DNB) (2016), "The AFM and DNB are easing access to the market with 'regulatory sandbox'", Press Release, 21 December (www.dnb.nl/en/news/news-and-archive/persberichten-2016/dnb350710.jsp).

EBA (2016), "On the draft Regulatory Technical Standards specifying the requirements on strong customer authentication and common and secure communication under PSD2", Consultation Paper EBA-CP-2016-11, 12 August (www.eba.europa.eu/documents/10180/1548183/Consultation+Paper+on+draft+RTS+on+SCA+and+CSC+(EBA-CP-2016-11).pdf).

ESMA (2014), "Investment-based crowdfunding", Opinion, December (www.esma.europa.eu/sites/default/files/library/2015/11/2014-1378_opinion_on_investment-based_crowdfunding.pdf).

European Commission (1998), Directive 98/6/EC of the European Parliament and of the Council on consumer protection in the indication of the prices of products offered to consumers, 16 February (http://eur-lex.europa.eu/resource.html?uri=cellar:b8fd669f-e013-4f8a-a9e1-2ff0dfee7de6.0008.02/DOC_1&format=PDF).

European Commission (2000), Directive 2000/31/EC of the European Parliament and of the Council on certain legal aspects of information society services, in particular electronic commerce, in the Internal Market (Directive on electronic commerce), 8 June (http://eur-lex.europa.eu/legal-content/EN/TXT/PDF/?uri=CELEX:32000L0031&from=EN).

European Commission (2002), Directive 2002/65/EC of the European Parliament and of the Council concerning the distance marketing of consumer financial services and amending Council Directive 90/619/EEC and Directives 97/7/EC and 98/27/EC, 23 September (http://eur-lex.europa.eu/legal-content/EN/TXT/PDF/?uri=CELEX:32002L0065&from=EN).

European Commission (2005), Directive 2005/29/EC of the European Parliament and of the Council concerning unfair business-to-consumer commercial practices in the internal market and amending Council Directive 84/450/EEC, Directives 97/7/EC, 98/27/EC and 2002/65/EC of the European Parliament and of the Council and Regulation (EC) No 2006/2004 of the European Parliament and of the Council ('Unfair Commercial Practices Directive'), 11 May (http://eur-lex.europa.eu/LexUriServ/LexUriServ.do?uri=OJ:L:2005:149:0022:0039:EN:PDF).

European Commission (2006a), Directive 2006/114/EC of the European Parliament and of the Council concerning misleading and comparative advertising, 12 December (http://eur-lex.europa.eu/legal-content/EN/TXT/PDF/?uri=CELEX:32006L0114&from=EN).

European Commission (2006b), Directive 2006/123/EC of the European Parliament and of the Council on services in the internal market, 12 December (http://eur-lex.europa.eu/legal-content/EN/TXT/PDF/?uri=CELEX:32006L0123&from=EN).

European Commission (2008), Directive 2008/48/EC of the European Parliament and of the Council on credit agreements for consumers and repealing Council Directive 87/102/EEC, 23 April (http://eur-lex.europa.eu/LexUriServ/LexUriServ.do?uri=OJ:L:2008:133:0066:0092: EN:PDF).

European Commission (2009), Communication from the Commission to the Council and the European Parliament - Review of the Distance Marketing of Consumer Financial Services Directive (2002/65/EC), 23 November (http://ec.europa.eu/consumers/archive/rights/docs/com_review_dis tance_mark_cfsd_en.pdf).

European Commission (2011a), Directive 2011/83/EU of the European Parliament and of the Council on consumer rights, amending Council Directive 93/13/EEC and Directive 1999/44/EC of the European Parliament and of the Council and repealing Council Directive 85/577/EEC and Directive 97/7/EC of the European Parliament and of the Council, 25 October (http://eur-lex.europa.eu/legal-content/EN/ TXT/PDF/?uri=CELEX:32011L0083&from=EN).

European Commission (2011b), Directive 2011/90/EU amending Part II of Annex I to Directive 2008/48/EC of the European Parliament and of the Council providing additional assumptions for the calculation of the annual percentage rate of charge, 14 November (http://eur-lex.europa.eu/LexUriServ/LexUriServ.do?uri=OJ:L:2011:296:0035:0037: EN:PDF).

European Commission (2012), Regulation of the European Parliament and of the Council on the protection of individuals with regard to the processing of personal data and on the free movement of such data (General Data Protection Regulation), SEC(2012) 72 final} {SEC(2012) 73 final}, 25 January (http://eurlex.europa.eu/legal-content/EN/TXT/PDF/?uri= CELEX:52012PC0011&from=en).

European Commission (2014a), Directive 2014/17/EU of the European Parliament and of the Council on credit agreements for consumers relating to residential immovable property and amending Directives 2008/48/EC and 2013/36/EU and Regulation (EU) No 1093/2010, 4 February (http://eur-lex.europa.eu/legal-content/EN/TXT/PDF/?uri= CELEX:32014L0017&from=EN).

European Commission (2014b), Directive 2014/92/EU of the European Parliament and of the Council on the comparability of fees related to payment accounts, payment account switching and access to payment accounts with basic features, 23 July (http://eur-lex.europa.eu/legal-content/EN/TXT/PDF/?uri=CELEX:32014L0092&from=en).

European Commission (2015a), "Evaluation and Fitness Check Roadmap" (http://ec.europa.eu/smart-regulation/roadmaps/docs/2015_sante_ 595_evaluation_health_claims_en.pdf).

European Commission (2015b), Directive (EU) 2015/2366 of the European Parliament and of the Council on payment services in the internal market, amending Directives 2002/65/EC, 2009/110/EC and 2013/36/EU and Regulation (EU) No 1093/2010, and repealing Directive 2007/64/EC, 25 November (http://eur-lex.europa.eu/legal-content/EN/TXT/PDF/?uri=CELEX:32015L2366&from=EN).

European Commission (2015c), Directive (EU) 2015/849 of the European Parliament and of the Council on the prevention of the use of the financial system for the purposes of money laundering or terrorist financing, amending Regulation (EU) No 648/2012 of the European Parliament and of the Council, and repealing Directive 2005/60/EC of the European Parliament and of the Council and Commission Directive 2006/70/EC, 20 May (http://eur-lex.europa.eu/legal-content/EN/TXT/PDF/?uri=OJ:JOL_2015_141_R_0003&from=ES).

European Commission (2016), Directive (EU) 2016/97 of the European Parliament and of the Council on insurance distribution (recast), 20 January (http://eur-lex.europa.eu/legal-content/EN/TXT/PDF/?uri=CELEX:32016L0097&from=EN).

European Data Protection Supervisor (EDPS) (2015), "Towards a new digital ethics: Data, dignity and technology", Opinion 4/2015, 11 September (https://secure.edps.europa.eu/EDPSWEB/webdav/site/mySite/shared/Documents/Consultation/Opinions/2015/15-09-11_Data_Ethics_EN.pdf).

Ezrachi, A. and M.E. Stucke (2016), "The rise of behavioural discrimination", Oxford Legal Studies Research Paper No. 54/2016 (https://papers.ssrn.com/sol3/papers.cfm?abstract_id=2830206).

Financial Conduct Authority (FCA) (2015a), "Regulatory sandbox", PUB REF: 005147, London, November (www.fca.org.uk/publication/research/regulatory-sandbox.pdf).

Financial Conduct Authority (FCA) (2015b), "Regulatory sandbox", webpage, 11 May, updated 1 February 2017 (www.fca.org.uk/firms/project-innovate-innovation-hub/regulatory-sandbox).

Finextra (2016), "Thailand sets up fintech sandbox", blogpost, 22 September (www.finextra.com/newsarticle/29475/thailand-sets-up-fintech-sandbox).

FINMA (2016), "FINMA reduces obstacles to FinTech", News, para. 3, 17 March (www.finma.ch/en/news/2016/03/20160317-mm-fintech/).

Google (2015), Google Barometer (www.consumerbarometer.com/en).

Joint Committee of the European Supervisory Authorities (2016), "The use of big data by financial institutions", Joint Committee Discussion Paper, December (www.esma.europa.eu/sites/default/files/library/jc-2016-86_discussion_paper_big_data.pdf)

Jolls, C., C.R. Sunstein and R. Thaler (2000), "A Behavioral Approach to Law and Economics", in CR. Sunstein (ed.), *Behavioral Law and Economics*, Cambridge: Cambridge University Press.

Linde, U. (2016), "EIDAS in the European Financial Sector: Use Cases and Compliance", Presentation, 19 September (www.tuvit.de/cps/rde/xbcr/SID-FE0F8F47-1BA1C05D/tuevit_de/ca-day-2016-linde-ulrike.pdf).

Martin, K.E. (2015), "Ethical Issues in the Big Data Industry", *MIS Quarterly Executive*, Vol. 14, No. 2, p. 74.

Milne, A. and P. Parboteeah (2016), "The Business Models and Economics of Peer-to-Peer Lending", ECRI Research Report No. 17, May (www.ecri.eu/new/node/424).

Monetary Authority of Singapore (MAS) (2016a), "Fintech Regulatory Sandbox Guidelines", Consultation Paper P005, 6 June (www.mas.gov.sg/~/media/MAS/News%20and%20Publications/Consultation%20Papers/Consultation%20Paper%20on%20FinTech%20Regulatory%20Sandbox%20Guidelines.pdf).

Monetary Authority of Singapore (MAS) (2016b), "Fintech Regulatory Sandbox Guidelines", November (www.mas.gov.sg/~/media/Smart%20Financial%20Centre/Sandbox/FinTech%20Regulatory%20Sandbox%20Guidelines.pdf).

Pinsent Masons (2016), "Hong Kong to create sandbox for financial services technology", Out-law.com: Legal news and guidance from Pinsent Masons (law firm), Special Report, 7 September (www.out-law.com/en/articles/2016/september/hong-kong-to-create-sandbox-for-financial-services-technology/).

Ranyard, R. (2014), "Cost disclosure in the retail credit market: research and policy implications", ECRI News, Autumn Edition, No. 46, p. 2 (www.ecri.be/new/system/files/14Nov14%20-%20%20ECRI%20Newsletter-_0.pdf).

Wagner, B. (2016), "Etikk I praksis", *Nordic Journal of Applied Ethics*, No. 1, pp. 5-13 (www.ntnu.no/ojs/index.php/etikk_i_praksis/article/view/1961).

ANNEX. TASK FORCE MEMBERS AND INVITED SPEAKERS

Chair: **Kim Vindberg-Larsen**
FinTech Entrepreneur

Rapporteur: **Sylvain Bouyon**
Research Fellow, CEPS and ECRI

Task Force Members

Javier Arias, Group Head EU Affairs, BBVA

Sue Basu, Senior Policy Advisor, Visa Europe

Christophe Bonte, Senior Adviser, Swiss Finance Council

Marco Boscolo, Policy Adviser, International and Regulatory Affairs Department, Intesa Sanpaolo

Axel Bysikiewicz, Head of Corporate Governance, Schufa Holding AG

Anne Chauviré, Senior Adviser, BNP Paribas

Jean-Eric De Mesmay, Director Institutional Relations, Cofidis

Raffaella Donnini, Director of the European Growth Policies Office, International and Regulatory Affairs Department, Intesa Sanpaolo

Sergey Filippov, Associate Director, Lisbon Council

Judith Hardt, Managing Director, Swiss Finance Council

Brit Hecht, EU Affairs Manager, BBVA

Tilman Hengevoss, Head of Public Affairs, EMEA, Zurich Insurance Company

Michael Hopp, Referent, Regulatory Department, Verband der Sparda-Banken e.V.

Olivier Jérusalmy, Managing Director, European Financial Inclusion Network (EFIN)

Simone Kayser, Retail Banking Adviser, Luxembourg Bankers Association

Sabine Malik, Senior Manager, Strategic Projects Executive Board, Schufa Holding AG

Otso Manninen, Economist, Bank of Finland

Monica Monaco, Founder and Managing Director, TrustEuAffairs

Noémie Papp, Digital & Retail Senior Policy Adviser, European Banking Federation

Lucia Pecchini, Regulatory Advisor, International and Regulatory Affairs Department, Intesa Sanpaolo

David Postius, Public Policy Analyst, EU Corporate Affairs, Banco Santander

David Rees, Director of Legal Affairs, Provident Financial

Ute Schmaltz, Advisor on European Affairs, Commerzbank AG

Michael Stephan, Chief Operating Officer and Founder, Raisin

Paul Thomalla, Global Head of Corporate Relations and Development, ACI Worldwide

Fabian Von Busse, Legal Adviser, MasterCard

Observers from the European Institutions

Elena Alampi, Policy Officer, eGovernment and Trust, DG CONNECT, European Commission

Guido Faltoni, Economist, European Central Bank

Jan-Martin Frie, Economic Analyst, European Political Strategy Centre, European Commission

Philippe Lefebvre, Head of Sector, Network Technologies Unit, DG CONNECT, European Commission

Andrea Servida, Head of Unit "eGovernment and Trust", DG CONNECT, European Commission

Stefano Spinaci, Financial Administrator, DG Finance, European Parliament

Saskia Stolk, Political Administrator, Council of the European Union

Invited Speakers

Kick-off meeting: 14 September 2016 – Definition of the scope

Olivier Denecker, Director of Knowledge, Global Payment Services, McKinsey & Company

Alistair Milne, Professor of Financial Economics, Loughborough School of Business and Economics

Olivier Salles, Head of Retail Financial Services and Payments, European Commission, DG FISMA

Second meeting: 8 November 2016 – Focus on Chapters 1 & 2

Fergal Carton, Lecturer and Researcher, University College Cork

J.B. McCarthy, Development Director, Financial Services Innovation Centre, University College Cork

Maria Lissowska, Senior Expert, Consumer Policy, DG Justice & Consumers, European Commission

Michael Pearson, Founder and CEO, Clarus Investments

Third meeting: 8 December 2016 – Focus on Chapters 3 & 4

Christoph Busch, Professor, European Legal Studies Institute, University of Osnabrück

Andrea Servida, Head of Unit "eGovernment and Trust", DG CONNECT, European Commission

Michael Stephan, Chief Operating Officer and Founder, Raisin

Fourth meeting: 31 December 2016– finalisation of the report

David Geale, Director of Policy, Financial Conduct Authority

www.ingramcontent.com/pod-product-compliance
Lightning Source LLC
Chambersburg PA
CBHW020358270326

41926CB00007B/486